Masters: Woodturning

DONALD DERRY ■ BEN CARPENTER ■
MICHAEL BAUERMEISTER ■ RON GERTON
■ MARK SFIRRI ■ MICHELLE HOLZAPFEL ■
J. PAUL FENNELL ■ GRAEME PRIDDLE
■ HANS WEISSFLOG ■ BINH PHO ■ MALCOLM TIBBETTS ■
ALAIN MAILLAND ■ CLAY FOSTER
■ GERRIT VAN NESS ■ CHRISTIAN BURCHARD ■
HUGH MCKAY ■ MARILYN CAMPBELL
■ STEPHEN HATCHER ■ JOHN JORDAN ■

MICHAEL HOSALUK ■ WILLIAM MOORE
■ DAVID ELLSWORTH ■ STEPHEN HOGBIN ■
RON LAYPORT ■ WILLIAM HUNTER ■ RON FLEMING
■ BUD LATVEN ■ JACQUES VESERY ■ BETTY SCARPINO ■
JEAN-FRANÇOIS ESCOULEN ■ STEVE SINNER
■ GILES GILSON ■ BERT MARSH ■ BRENDA BEHRENS ■
DAVID SENGEL ■ ALAN STIRT ■ MICHAEL BROLLY
■ BILL LUCE ■ CINDY DROZDA ■ MICHAEL LEE

Masters: Woodturning

Major Works by Leading Artists
Curated by Jim Christiansen

LARK BOOKS
A Division of Sterling Publishing Co., Inc.
New York / London

SENIOR EDITOR:
Suzanne J. E. Tourtillott

EDITOR:
Julie Hale

ART DIRECTOR:
Megan Kirby

ART PRODUCTION:
Jeff Hamilton

COVER DESIGNER:
Kay Holmes Stafford

FRONT COVER, LEFT TO RIGHT
Michael Hosaluk
Bird Vase, 2007
Photo by AK Photos

William Moore
Nehalem Vessel, 2005
Photo by Dan Kvitka

Michael Bauermeister
Forest Pond, 2007
Photo by artist

William Moore
Lidded Orb, 2006
Photo by Dan Kvitka

Binh Pho
Dreamer, 2007
Photo by artist

BACK COVER, LEFT TO RIGHT
Cindy Drozda
Space Station, 2004
Photo by Tim Benko

Jacques Vesery
Endless Currents, 2004
Photo by artist

Ben Carpenter
Elk Bowl, 2006
Photo by Powell

SPINE
Graeme Priddle
Eclipse, 1994
Photo by artist

Library of Congress Cataloging-in-Publication Data

Masters. Woodturning : major works by leading artists / [curated by Jim Christiansen;senior editor, Suzanne J.E. Tourtillott]. -- 1st ed.
    p. cm.
  Includes index.
  ISBN 978-1-60059-168-6 (pb-pbk. with flaps : alk. paper)
  1. Art woodwork--History--21st century--Catalogs. 2. Turning (Lathe work)--History--21st century--Catalogs. I. Tourtillott, Suzanne J. E. II. Title: Woodturning.

  NK9610.6.M37 2009
  745.51092'2--dc22
                                        2008023393

10 9 8 7 6 5 4 3 2 1

First Edition

Published by Lark Books, A Division of
Sterling Publishing Co., Inc.
387 Park Avenue South, New York, NY 10016

Text © 2009, Lark Books
Photography © 2009, Artist/Photographer

Distributed in Canada by Sterling Publishing,
c/o Canadian Manda Group, 165 Dufferin Street
Toronto, Ontario, Canada M6K 3H6

Distributed in the United Kingdom by GMC Distribution Services,
Castle Place, 166 High Street, Lewes, East Sussex, England BN7 1XU

Distributed in Australia by Capricorn Link (Australia) Pty Ltd.,
P.O. Box 704, Windsor, NSW 2756 Australia

If you have questions or comments about this book, please contact:
Lark Books, 67 Broadway
Asheville, NC 28801
828-253-0467

Manufactured in China

ISBN 13: 978-1-60059-168-6

For information about custom editions, special sales, premium and corporate purchases, please contact Sterling Special Sales Department at 800-805-5489 or specialsales@sterlingpub.com.

Contents

Introduction

WOODTURNING has undergone a great transformation. Only in the last 25 years has the wood lathe, formerly used to create utilitarian objects or furniture parts, served as a tool in the hands of the artist. While a handful of turners experimented and created very sophisticated work as early as the 1960s, their circle of influence was small. Then, under the guidance of a few visionaries, the American Association of Woodturners was established. Its annual symposium, along with the Utah Woodturning Symposium, gave expressive turners a forum and a means to communicate with each other. Those events led to an increased interest in turning by a growing number of people. Publications appeared, then gallery exhibitions. Today, the process is accelerating even faster, with a veritable explosion of new ideas coming from all over the world.

In this book you'll find an international collection of work displaying innovative ideas contributed by pioneering artists who have expanded our notions of what is possible with the lathe-turned wood form. Given the huge amount of creative work currently being done, selecting just 40 innovators was a challenging task. It is my hope that the groundbreaking work assembled here will provide a source for study, enlightenment, and enjoyment for aspiring artists as well as for those who take pleasure in seeing outstanding art.

A number of turners show us that even subtle changes in line and shape can make a great difference in a finished piece. Bill Luce, who has obsessively explored the many variations possible in a simple calabash bowl form, has given us examples so that we can see the difference between forms that are very good and those that are stunning. Bert Marsh provides a similar lesson with more complex re-curve bowl shapes. John Jordan and David Ellsworth have explored enclosed vessels, teaching us that achieving purity and beauty in classical forms is indeed a complex challenge.

Only recently, adding color and texture to wood creations was considered radical, almost destructive. Michael Hosaluk demonstrates otherwise. His paint and surface decorations are exciting design elements. As a result of such pioneering work, the use of color and the alteration of natural surfaces are now widely employed techniques. Giles Gilson and Don Derry produce work that is often mistaken for glass or fine china. Building on decorative traditions already established in the ceramic arts, Marilyn Campbell and Alan Stirt have devised new ways to enhance wood surfaces. It is clear that in addition to exploring new finishing methods, these turners have broken with tradition and set an example for others to follow in developing even more new ways to create turned art.

The use of the lathe to create sculpture is now a major part of the current design scene. Moving even further away from the tradition of creating utilitarian objects is abstract sculpture, which has become another key development. A wide variety of new ideas are being explored, ranging from the whimsical lathe-based works of Jean-François Escoulen and the spectacular high-energy work of newcomer Ben Carpenter to Betty Scarpino's refined and graceful pieces. Due to the efforts of these and other artists, it is now acceptable in the woodturning community to make objects that can be appreciated purely for their aesthetic value.

Carving is one of the oldest ways to enhance a turned object. Going beyond traditional techniques and discovering new ways to combine carving and turning have been some of the most significant developments of the last few years. Michelle Holzapfel's complex carved works demonstrate a broad understanding of composition. Ron Layport creates carved works in which repetition and abstract figures are used effectively as design elements. Brenda Behrens's carving connects us with the power of the medium and of Gaia. The expressive range of carved elements shown by many others in this collection attests not only to the popularity of the practice but to the seemingly endless number of new concepts being explored.

Finally, I considered emotional content when selecting the work for this volume. Many artists have found in the woodturning process a way to express their joy, their angst, their very souls. Indeed, in order to make the pieces shown in this book, the artists were heavily invested in the creative process. Some work is particularly effective in giving us a look at the thoughts and feelings of the maker. Gerrit Van Ness's work prods, angers, and humors us. His pieces also display exquisite form, composition, and

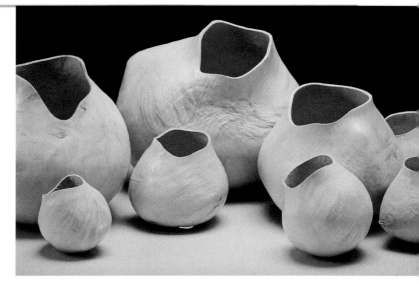

▲ **Christian Burchard**
Untitled | 2005

craftsmanship. Binh Pho reveals his heart and feelings in masterful presentations utilizing form, color, piercing, and symbols. Finding ways to express feelings in turned creations clearly represents the next design frontier.

As a survey of contemporary woodturning, this book provides an overview of work from the best artists participating in the medium today. Their pieces are rooted in tradition but clearly influenced by new design trends. Selecting these masters was a pleasure and a privilege, and I am proud to share their work with you.

—Jim Christiansen

Donald Derry

AN EXPERT MANIPULATOR OF TEXTURE AND FORM, Donald Derry creates pieces that are often mistaken for glass. He highlights the natural beauty of his material by using bright colors to accentuate grain patterns. To add color, Derry uses pigments from an industrial paint supplier. He rubs the pigments by hand into the wood, sands the piece to achieve the appropriate contrast, and adds solvent. He then sprays the form with several coats of water white lacquer, and polishes the surface by hand until it's optically perfect. On closer inspection, the natural grain and smooth finish of the wood add depth to Derry's creations. His large-scale pieces are vibrant and dramatic, with flowing sculptural details. Derry's work serves as a bridge, allowing us to experience both the beauty of wood and the essence of forms found in the natural world.

◀ **Island Woman** | 2004
24 x 10½ x 10½ inches
(61 x 26.7 x 26.7 cm)
Elm
Photo by artist

▲ **Untitled** | 2005

22½ x 9½ x 9½ inches
(57.2 x 24.1 x 24.1 cm)
Elm

Photo by artist

▲ **For Melony** | 2004

8 x 4 x 4 inches
(20.3 x 10.2 x 10.2 cm)
Box elder

Photo by artist

▲ **Mother and Daughters** | 2002

17 x 12 x 7 inches
(43.2 x 30.5 x 17.8 cm)
Maple
Photo by artist

Big Island Fire | 2006 ▶

38 x 13 x 13 inches
(96.5 x 33 x 33 cm)
Bigleaf maple
Photo by artist

◀ **Life Can Be Hard** | 2007

23 x 10 x 12 inches
(58.4 x 25.4 x 30.5 cm)
Maple burl

Photo by artist

" Most of my woodturning heroes worked with
color only to give it up because the public rejected
the coloring of wood. People seem to feel it's a
sacrilege to change the natural beauty of wood. "

" Way back in the flamboyant 1970s, I put hot-rod finishes on the custom rock-and-roll guitars I built. It seems only natural that my music background would find a place in my present work. "

▲ Fire Dance | 2006
5 x 4½ x 4½ inches
(12.7 x 11.4 x 11.4 cm)
Box elder
Photo by artist

Wind Horse | 2004 ▶
30 x 10 x 10 inches
(76.2 x 25.4 x 25.4 cm)
Elm
Photo by artist

DONALD DERRY

▲ Cincinnati Sunset | 2007

14 x 10 x 10 inches
(35.6 x 25.4 x 25.4 cm)
Elm

Photo by artist

American Chopper | 2003 ▶
16 x 18 x 16 inches
(40.6 x 45.7 x 40.6 cm)
Elm
Photo by artist

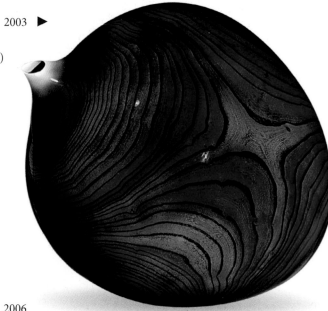

◀ **Red Bird** | 2006
25 x 18 x 8 inches
(63.5 x 45.7 x 20.3 cm)
Elm
Photo by artist

" Art needs to be hard—this is a truism
I use to keep myself honest. "

Life Long | 2006 ▶

16 x 11 x 8 inches
(40.6 x 27.9 x 20.3 cm)
Maple burl

Photo by artist

Ben Carpenter

PLAYFUL, INVENTIVE, AND BOLD, the work of Ben Carpenter features an incredible range of shapes and textures. Carpenter takes an ingenious approach to design, joining appendages and spikes to hollow forms and experimenting with carving techniques to accent turned pieces. His early work was shaped completely on the lathe, but recent pieces have been roughed out and carved by hand. Carpenter's ability to create logical, fluid curves is apparent even in the smallest details of his work. The design elements flow together, creating a wonderful sense of unity. His stand-alone sculptures are remarkable for their display of wood grain—evidence of Carpenter's ability to get the most out of his material. With an aesthetic that's dynamic and lively, Carpenter brings a unique vision to the world of woodturning.

◄ **Azurescens** | 2007
8 x 10 x 6 inches
(20.3 x 25.4 x 15.2 cm)
Maple burl, ebony
Photo by Powell

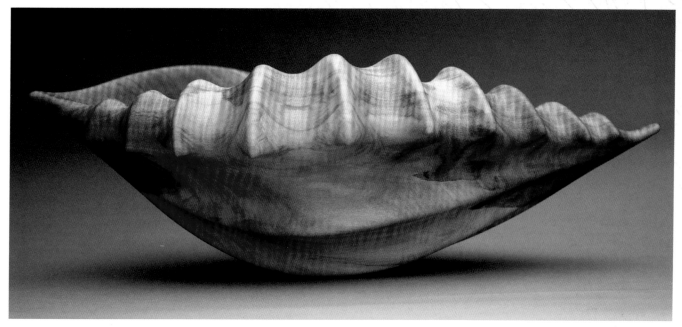

▲ **Panther** | 2007

6 x 16 x 10 inches
(15.2 x 40.6 x 25.4 cm)
Fiddleback maple

Photo by Powell

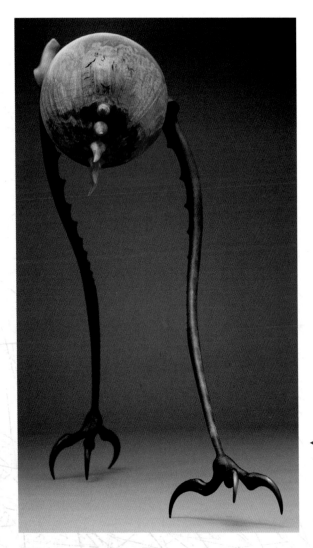

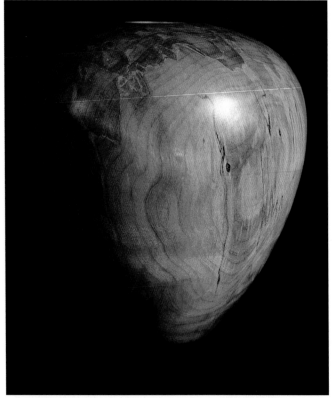

▲ **Subtle Flare** │ 1999

9 x 7 x 7 inches
(22.9 x 17.8 x 17.8 cm)
Birch

Photo by Will Simpson

◄ **Strider** │ 2006

33 x 16 x 24 inches
(83.8 x 40.6 x 61 cm)
Walnut burl, camphor burl,
Macassar ebony, maple

Photo by Powell

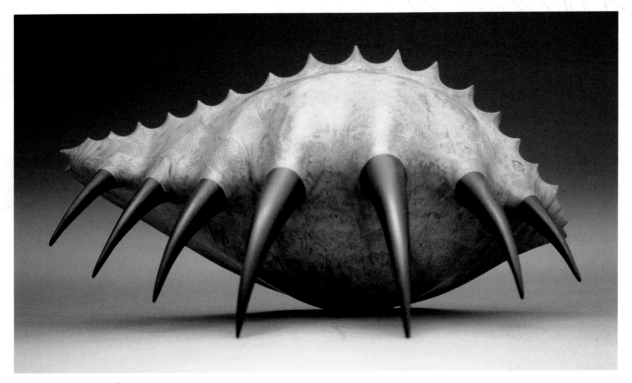

▲ **Black Orchid** | 2006

12 x 16 x 9 inches
(30.5 x 40.6 x 22.9 cm)
Black locust, ebony

Photo by Powell

" I prefer solitude for the idea phase of my

work and camaraderie for its execution. "

▲ Nocturnal Concentration | 2005

10 x 8 x 8 inches
(25.4 x 20.3 x 20.3 cm)
Maple burl

Photo by Powell

▲ Archaic Submarine | 2005

12 x 11 x 11 inches
(30.5 x 27.9 x 27.9 cm)
Walnut burl, maple burl

Photo by Powell

◀ **Coriolis** │ 2007

28 x 30 x 8 inches
(71.1 x 76.2 x 20.3 cm)
Maple burl
Photo by Powell

◀ **Culminar II** │ 2007

16 x 10 x 9 inches
(40.6 x 25.4 x 22.9 cm)
Maple burl
Photo by Powell

" Even in woodturning, where the basic variable is a two-dimensional line,
the possibilities can be overwhelming to me. Because of this, I try to pick
an idea and run with it, not stopping until the idea has become a reality. **"**

Eolian Drifting Pod | 2006 ▶

10 x 17 x 6 inches
(25.4 x 43.2 x 15.2 cm)
Maple burl

Photo by Powell

▲ **Triskelion** | 2003

8 x 16 x 4½ inches
(20.3 x 40.6 x 11.4 cm)
Walnut

Photo by Powell

▲ **Dragon's Egg** | 2006

15 x 10 x 10 inches
(38.1 x 25.4 x 25.4 cm)
Maple burl

Photo by Powell

" The ideas of natural geometry, the golden mean,
and Fibonacci sequences have always intrigued
me, and now they come through in my work. "

Michael Bauermeister

A PRODUCER OF LARGE, MAJESTIC SCULPTURES, Michael Bauermeister creates pieces that have a special presence—vases and vessels that would be suitable in a setting where sacred rituals take place. Creating large-scale works presents unique challenges, and Bauermeister meets them by drawing on his previous experience as a furniture maker and sculptor. He uses a bandsaw extensively, and the lamination process provides a starting point for many of his pieces. The use of both traditional carving gouges and power tools allows him to engage in wide-ranging explorations of texture, form, and scale. Bauermeister also plays with color in his work, often contrasting the natural hue of polished wood with bright paint. Bauermeister has said that he strives for natural beauty in his pieces. This aesthetic definitely shines through in his work, from delicate sculptural objects to tall, robust vessels.

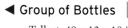

◀ Group of Bottles | 2006

Tallest, 49 x 12 x 10 inches
(124.5 x 30.5 x 25.4 cm)
Linden

Photo by artist

▲ Arc Vessels | 2004

Each, 15 x 15 x 9 inches
(38.1 x 38.1 x 22.9 cm)
Maple, cherry

Photo by artist

▲ **Eccentricity** | 2006
39 x 10 x 10 inches
(99.1 x 25.4 x 25.4 cm)
Pine

Photo by artist

▲ **Winter Branches** | 2007
38 x 15 x 15 inches
(96.5 x 38.1 x 38.1 cm)
Kentucky coffee tree

Photo by artist

" Somewhere between a tree and a wooden vase, where the hand of the artist and the hand of God are both evident—that's the point that interests me. "

◀ **Two Incised Vessels** | 2005

Tallest, 39 x 12 inches
(99.1 x 30.5 cm)
Maple, walnut

Photo by artist

▲ **Group of Sprout Vessels** | 2003

Tallest, 36 inches (91.4 cm)
Various hardwoods

Photo by artist

▲ **Two Sprout Vessels** | 2005

Tallest, 39 x 10 inches
(99.1 x 25.4 cm)
Pine, maple

Photo by artist

" I have the same reaction to finding a beautiful wasp's nest that I do to finding a well-designed spoon. Both have intent, purpose, and form. I would like my work to be something you find that makes you wonder if it was made by a wasp or a person. "

◀ **Holy and Unholy** | 2006
45 x 19 x 14 inches
(114.3 x 48.3 x 35.6 cm)
Oak
Photo by artist

MICHAEL BAUERMEISTER

▲ **Wound-Up** | 2007

51 x 14 x 14 inches
(129.5 x 35.6 x 35.6 cm)
Linden

Photo by artist

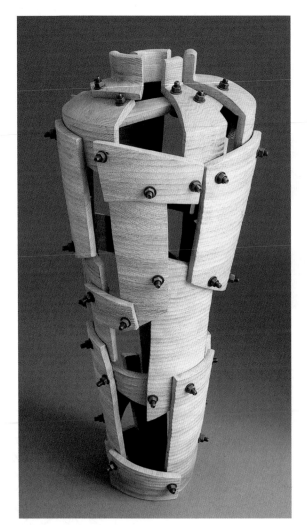

▲ **Tikun Vessel** | 2006

38 x 12 x 12 inches
(96.5 x 30.5 x 30.5 cm)
Oak

Photo by artist

▲ **Bundle** | 2002

40 x 19 x 19 inches
(101.6 x 48.3 x 48.3 cm)
Oak

Photo by artist

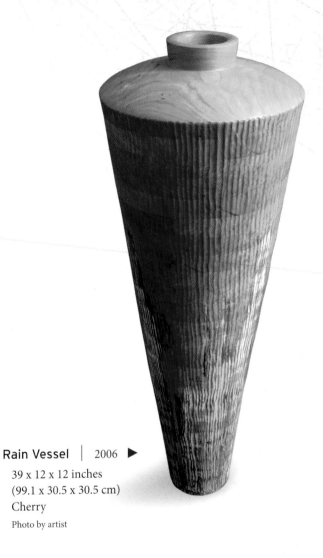

Rain Vessel | 2006 ▶

39 x 12 x 12 inches
(99.1 x 30.5 x 30.5 cm)
Cherry

Photo by artist

" Wood has become my voice and my language. Sometimes everything comes together into a kind of wooden poem. "

Ron Gerton

COMBINING THE EYE OF AN ENGINEER WITH THE HEART OF AN ARTIST, Ron Gerton has produced a diverse body of work that reflects both facets of his personality. His closed vessels are dramatically twisted shapes that reveal the possibilities hidden within a simple form. Drawing on his experience as an engineer, Gerton has developed equipment that allows him to turn and hollow vessels up to eight feet in diameter. Other pieces feature the wood remains of dead sagebrush, which Gerton transforms into bronze by using a ceramic material capable of withstanding high temperatures. Striking a complex balance between proportion and distortion, these bronze and wood pieces reflect the eternal struggle for survival that takes place in nature. Gerton, an experimenter who believes the spectrum of design is unlimited, creates innovative work that demonstrates his versatility as an artist.

◀ Wood You Marry Me? | 2006
24 x 18 x 9 inches
(61 x 45.7 x 22.9 cm)
Curly maple
Photo by artist

◀ **The Ants Go Marching** | 2007

27 x 20 x 16 inches
(68.6 x 50.8 x 40.6 cm)
Maple burl
Photo by artist

Desert Dancer | 1997 ▶

48 x 23 x 34 inches
(121.9 x 58.4 x 86.4 cm)
Spalted maple burl

Photo by artist

◀ **Ripple** | 2002

15 x 18 x 16 inches
(38.1 x 45.7 x 40.6 cm)
Locust burl

Photo by artist

" I get great pleasure from creating
something just for the fun of it.
And that creation doesn't have to do
anything but stir up an emotional
response in the viewer—which isn't
as easy as it sounds. "

▲ Blossom, a Collaborative | 2005

14 x 12 x 9 inches
(35.6 x 30.5 x 22.9 cm)
Hackberry burl
Turned by Alain Mailland

Photo by artist

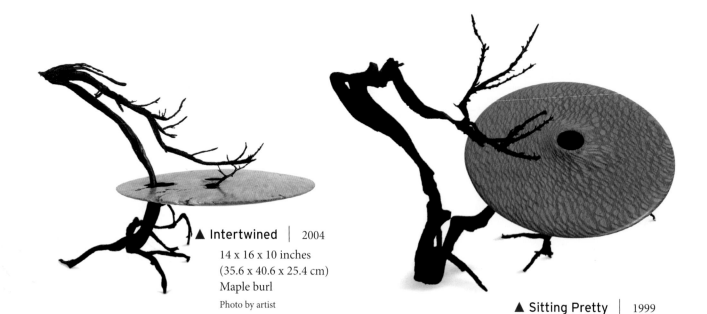

▲ **Intertwined** | 2004

14 x 16 x 10 inches
(35.6 x 40.6 x 25.4 cm)
Maple burl

Photo by artist

▲ **Sitting Pretty** | 1999

16 x 16 x 10 inches
(40.6 x 40.6 x 25.4 cm)
Lacewood

Photo by artist

▲ **Between a Rock and a Pretty Place** | 2007

13 x 18 x 14 inches
(33 x 45.7 x 35.6 cm)
Redwood

Photo by artist

" I live in the desert in
Washington State, where a
constant struggle for survival
can mold trees and shrubs into
natural bonsai. I collect these
decaying remains and give
them a permanence in bronze,
creating what I call 'bronzai.' "

◀ **Have a Heart** | 1998

18 x 13 x 13 inches
(45.7 x 33 x 33 cm)
Manzanita burl
Photo by artist

Evolution Revolution | 2005 ▶

38 x 26 x 10 inches
(96.5 x 66 x 25.4 cm)
Mango

Photo by artist

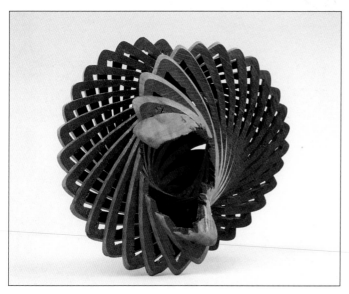

◀ Twister | 2003

12 x 12 x 10 inches
(30.5 x 30.5 x 25.4 cm)
Maple burl

Photo by artist

" Woodturning and bronze
casting have allowed me to
work on large-scale pieces.
To me, these pieces are
jewelry—jewelry for a space
rather than a body. "

◀ Good to the Last Drop | 2004

10 x 36 x 24 inches
(25.4 x 91.4 x 61 cm)
Curly maple

Photo by artist

Mark Sfirri

WHAT HE CALLS "SPONTANEOUS EXPLORATIONS OF FORM" have led Mark Sfirri to create his own kind of whimsical, free-spirited wooden sculptures. Known for his bold compositions and meticulous attention to detail, Sfirri creates furniture and sculptural objects that combine both concave and convex surfaces and feature beautifully shaped curvilinear contours. Sfirri's tables and benches sometimes have four different legs—a lack of uniformity that gives them an off-kilter charm. Breaking down the barriers that separate woodturning and sculpture, his work projects a sense of humor that's at once wry and enigmatic. By combining turning with carving or multi-axis turning, Sfirri is able to explore form in an uninhibited way. This approach has resulted in a body of work that's remarkable for its diversity and creativity.

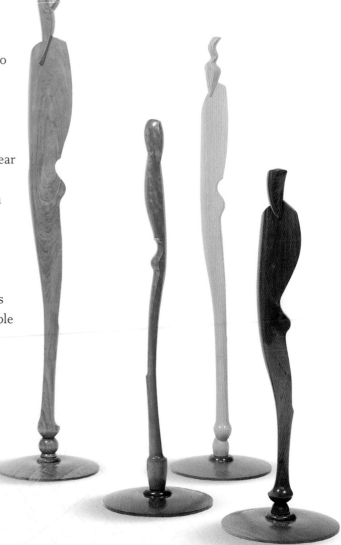

Glancing Figures | 1997 ▶

Tallest, 72 inches
(182.9 cm)
Cherry, ash, walnut

Photo by Randl Bye

◀ **Walking Table** | 1999
29 x 16½ x 21 inches
(73.7 x 41.9 x 53.3 cm)
Curly cherry, wenge
Photo by artist

" Before I start a new piece I think about the effect that I'm trying to achieve (the concept) and the geometry required to create it (the engineering). I enjoy the challenges of both. "

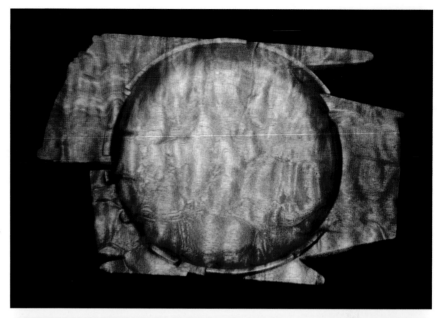

Quilted Quasar | 1986 ▶

2 x 12 x 8 inches
(5.1 x 30.5 x 20.3 cm)
Mahogany

Photo by artist

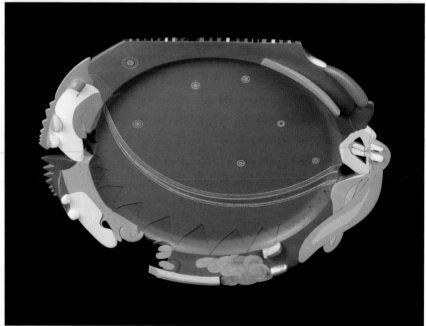

Bugs and Thugs | 1988 ▶

4 x 20 x 20 inches
(10.2 x 50.8 x 50.8 cm)
Poplar

Photo by artist

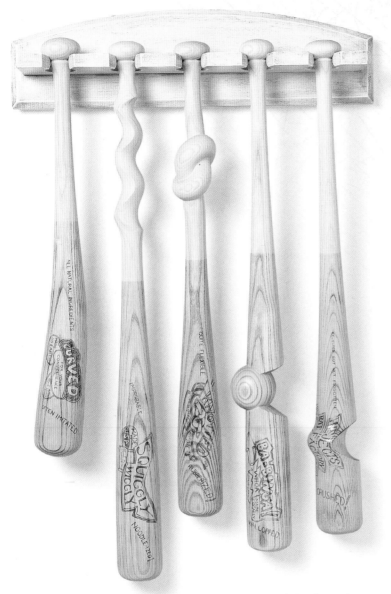

▲ **10th Anniversary–Rejects from the Bat Factory** | 2002

38 x 24 x 6 inches
(96.5 x 61 x 15.2 cm)
Ash

Photo by John Carlano

▲ **Madonna and Child Revisited** | 2003

Tallest, 20 1/2 inches
(52.1 cm)
Walnut

Photo by John Carlano

80 x 48 x 14 inches
(203.2 x 121.9 x 35.6 cm)
Ash

Photo by Randl Bye

" My work has almost exclusively been the result of spindle, or 'between center,' turning. Oftentimes, the final forms are far removed from the forms that are usually associated with the lathe. "

MARK **SFIRRI**

▲ **Logger Lager** | 2003

11 x 5 x 4 inches
(27.9 x 12.7 x 10.2 cm)
Poplar

Photo by John Carlano

Trois en Un | 2003 ▶

10 x 5 x 4 inches
(25.4 x 12.7 x 10.2 cm)
Poplar

Photo by John Carlano

The Little People | 2004 ▶

Tallest, 7¼ inches (18.4 cm)
Various hardwoods

Photo by John Carlano

◀ **Sea of Spoons** | 2006

Tallest, 4¾ inches (12.1 cm)
Miscellaneous hardwoods

Photo by John Carlano

" My interest in woodturning grew out of an interest in carving. Turning seemed like a challenging way to create pieces that weren't the round, symmetrical forms that are the obvious results of lathe work. "

◀ **Spider Table** | 1993
33 x 21 x 13 inches
(83.8 x 53.3 x 33 cm)
Lacewood, curly maple
Photo by Randl Bye

MARK SFIRRI

Michelle Holzapfel

USING TRADITIONAL THEMES IN WAYS THAT ARE FRESH AND UNEXPECTED, Michelle Holzapfel creates work that's characterized by her own kind of visual poetry. Inspired by images from daily life—textile, plant, animal, and human forms—Holzapfel emphasizes the tactile possibilities of wood as she carves. From smoothly pleated forms to basketweave motifs and corduroy-like surfaces, her pieces feature an incredible range of patterns and textures. Working with hardwoods abandoned in the wake of logging operations—burls, gnarled branches, and center-rotten trunks—she welcomes irregularities and extravagant grain patterns in wood. While her early vessels featured low-relief carvings, Holzapfel's recent creations are characterized by high-relief motifs that seem to rise from the surface of the work. Some pieces feature articulated forms that can actually move.

Ptolemy Vase | 1999 ▶

16 x 12 x 8 inches
(40.6 x 30.5 x 20.3 cm)
Spalted sugar maple,
yellow birch maple

Photo by David Holzapfel

◀ **Serpent Bowl** | 1998

4 x 16 x 16 inches
(10.2 x 40.6 x 40.6 cm)
Wild cherry burl

Photo by David Holzapfel

Knotted Handles Vase | 2006 ▶

16 x 16 x 6 inches
(40.6 x 40.6 x 15.2 cm)
Yellow birch burl

Photo by David Holzapfel

▲ **Birthday Cake** | 1986

10 x 16 x 16 inches
(25.4 x 40.6 x 40.6 cm)
Walnut, maple

Photo by David Holzapfel

▲ **Self-Portrait** | 1986

18 x 8 x 8 inches
(45.7 x 20.3 x 20.3 cm)
Wild cherry burl

Photo by David Holzapfel

◀ **Macedonia Vase** | 1986

14 x 14 x 4 inches
(35.6 x 35.6 x 10.2 cm)
American beech burl

Photo by David Holzapfel

" When learning to use my machinist's lathe, what I didn't know *didn't* hurt me. My father built the lathe, so it came with no instructions. Through trial and error, I devised my own method for manipulating the cutter. Ignorance has been a great ally ."

◀ Fibonacci Vase │ 1991

9 x 9 x 3 inches
(22.9 x 22.9 x 7.6 cm)
Sugar maple
Photo by David Holzapfel

MICHELLE HOLZAPFEL

" Like a good vintner, I hope to capture the *terroir*—the flavors of soil and climate embodied in wood. **"**

▲ Draped Bowl | 2005

8 x 16 x 16 inches
(20.3 x 40.6 x 40.6 cm)
Bleached yellow birch

Photo by David Holzapfel

▲ **Cushioned Bowl #2** | 1997

8 x 15 x 15 inches
(20.3 x 38.1 x 38.1 cm)
Fiddleback sugar maple

Photo by David Holzapfel

" No matter what form I might have 'in mind,'

it doesn't begin to live until I've experienced it 'in hand.' "

▲ **Suspended Ring Vase** | 1996

12 x 12 x 3 inches
(30.5 x 30.5 x 7.6 cm)
Sugar maple burl
Photo by David Holzapfel

▲ Domestic Violence 2 | 1988

30 x 18 x 14 inches
(76.2 x 45.7 x 35.6 cm)
Assorted hardwoods
Photo by David Holzapfel

▲ Ingenue Vase | 2000

10 x 6 x 6 inches
(25.4 x 15.2 x 15.2 cm)
Butternut, walnut
Photo by David Holzapfel

J. Paul Fennell

THE EXPRESSIVENESS OF HOLLOW FORMS has long been a point of focus for J. Paul Fennell. Precisely designed and carefully executed, his pieces have a special energy thanks to their pierced and carved surfaces. Fennell's exploration of patterns—Chinese lattice designs, floral motifs, and water imagery—reflects his breadth as an artist. His creations are complex, delicate, and made with the thinnest wood possible. Fennell makes his thin-walled vessels with the aid of a fiber optic light, which he places inside a form while he hollows it out. When the wood becomes translucent, Fennell knows it's sufficiently thin. To carve and pierce his pieces, he uses an air-driven dental lab handpiece and dental burs. The end result: vessels that are richly alive, teeming with a wonderful abundance of detail.

Fleurs et Vignes | 2002 ▶

8 x 6 inches
(20.3 x 15.2 cm)
Citrus

Photo by artist

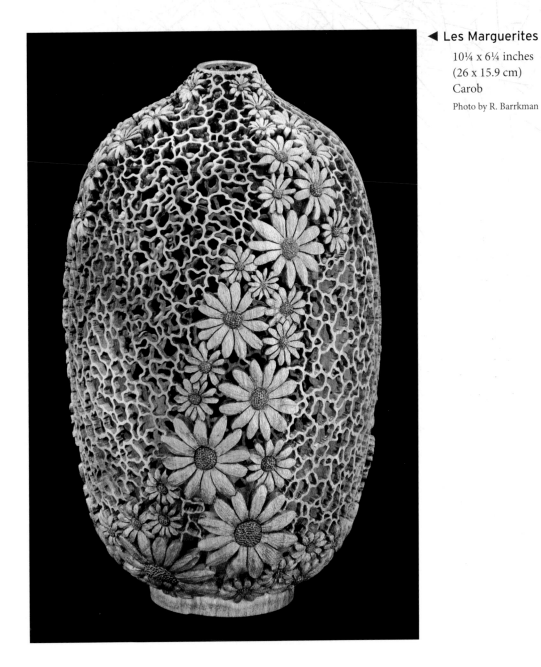

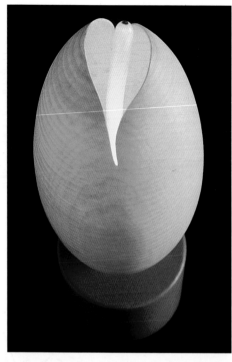

◀ **Fleur de Neon II** | 1991

11 x 4 inches
(27.9 x 10.2 cm)
Curly maple

Photo by artist

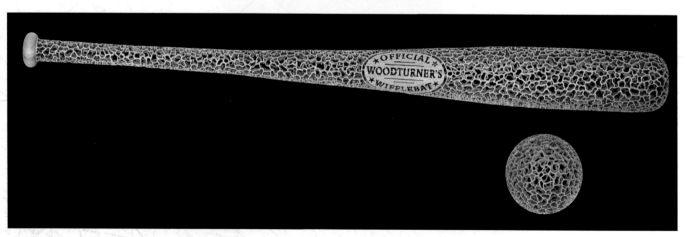

▲ **Official Woodturner's Wiffle Bat and Ball** | 2006

30 x 2¾ inches
(76.2 x 7 cm)
Mesquite

Photo by R. Barrkman

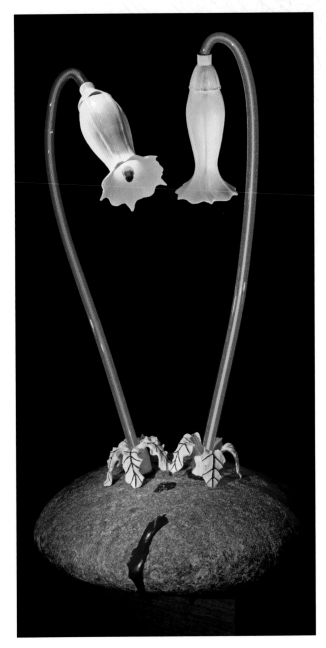

" Through the visual and tactile senses, an observer of my work is offered expressive links to my experiences in an easily understood 'language.' "

◀ **Blood from a Stone** | 2007

16 x 8 x 10 inches
(40.6 x 20.3 x 25.4 cm)
Citrus

Photo by R. Barrkman

▲ Discovery | 2002

9¼ x 10 inches
(23.5 x 25.4 cm)
Carob

Photo by R. Barrkman

▲ Fissures | 2007

5¼ x 5¾ inches
(13.3 x 14.6 cm)
Carob

Photo by artist

> *"* Most of my work concerns the aesthetics of the vessel form. The vessel is timeless and ubiquitous, a presence in a multitude of cultures, both past and present. *"*

▲ **Spirals** | 2007
6½ x 6½ inches
(16.5 x 16.5 cm)
Found wood
Photo by artist

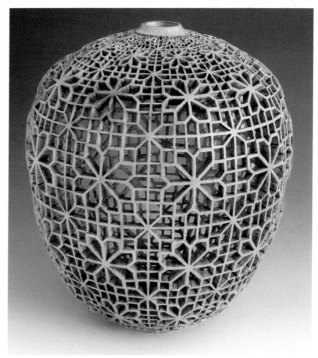

Omei | 2007 ▶
10 x 9 inches
(25.4 x 22.9 cm)
Mesquite
Photo by artist

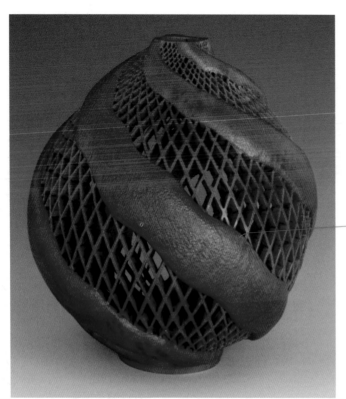

" Inspiration does not necessarily happen instantaneously. It's often diffused over time. It can soften the sharp edges of reality and make the essence of an idea more abstract. "

▲ **Lattice with Orange Peel** | 2006

7 x 6 inches
(17.8 x 15.2 cm)
African sumac
Photo by artist

View from the Garden | 2006 ▶

7½ x 6½ inches
(19.1 x 16.5 cm)
African sumac
Photo by artist

J. PAUL FENNELL

▲ **Red Cord Redux** | 2007

12½ x 9½ inches
(31.8 x 24.1 cm)
Carob

Photo by artist

Graeme Priddle

A NATIVE OF NEW ZEALAND, Graeme Priddle has long been inspired by the coastal and marine environments that surround him. Many of his turned and carved objects feature textures that bring to mind the ripples in a tide pool. Ocean motifs such as shells and starfish appear frequently in his work. Priddle created early pieces from decorative timber, keeping design to a minimum so as not to overshadow the natural beauty of the wood. With new pieces, however, design is usually the dominant factor. Vessels featuring dramatic surface decoration and texture were inspired by traditional Maori carvers, whose work Priddle admires. Turned pieces that have been cut apart and reassembled have the complex construction of wooden boats. Expertly designed and cleanly composed, Priddle's work feels fresh and modern, yet it's infused with a rich sense of history.

◀ Koru Chalice | 1994

19½ x 8½ inches
(49.5 x 21.6 cm)
Black maire
Photo by artist

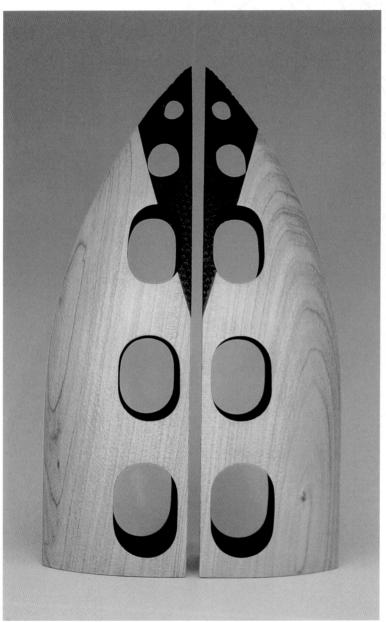

◀ **Reflection** | 2006

57 x 30 x 15 inches
(144.8 x 76.2 x 38.1 cm)
Monterey cypress
Photos by artist

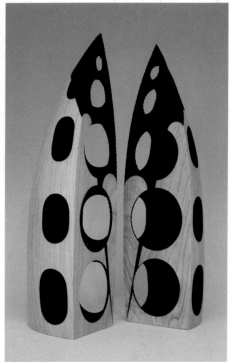

▲ Eclipse | 1994
36 x 34 x 19½ inches
(91.4 x 86.4 x 49.5 cm)
New Zealand kauri
Photo by artist

" One of the things that I like most about wood is that it's not a manufactured material. Each piece is like a recorded slice of history. "

◀ **Against the Tide** | 2001

29½ x 6 inches
(74.9 x 15.2 cm)
New Zealand kauri burr

Photo by artist

◀ **Tribute to George** | 2000

9 x 35½ x 12 inches
(22.9 x 90.2 x 30.5 cm)
Walnut

Photo by artist

▲ **Waka Pakake** | 2002

4½ x 44 x 7½ inches
(11.4 x 111.8 x 19.1 cm)
New Zealand matai
Photo by artist

" I find technical challenges to be a breeze
compared to creative challenges. I experienced
many years of frustration and producing bowls
before I discovered my own voice. *"*

Starfish Vessel | 2006 ▶

16½ x 11½ x 7 inches
(41.9 x 29.2 x 17.8 cm)
New Zealand kauri, ebony
Photo by artist

◀ **Outrigger Vessel** │ 2001

27 x 13 inches
(68.6 x 33 cm)
Monterey cypress burr, mulga
Photo by artist

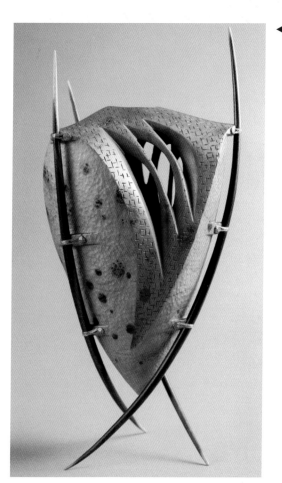

◀ **Point Break** │ 2006

26 x 11½ inches
(66 x 29.2 cm)
Monterey cypress, mulga
Photo by artist

Tangaroa's Gift | 2007 ▶

7 x 19 x 25 inches
(17.8 x 48.3 x 63.5 cm)
Jarrah burr

Photo by artist

◀ **Tangaroa's Gift** | 2007

9 x 21 x 28 inches
(22.9 x 53.3 x 71.1 cm)
Huon pine

Photo by artist

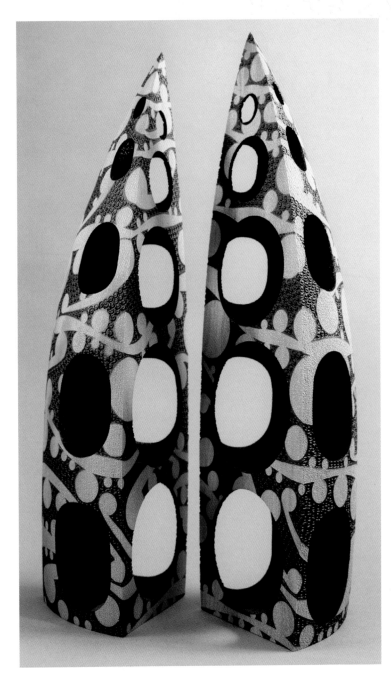

" The most important aspect of my work is that it tells stories. I'm not comfortable with embellishment for the sake of embellishment. Every detail of a piece must relate to the story that I'm telling. "

◀ Tahi, Rua | 2007
37½ x 19 x 10 inches
(95.3 x 48.3 x 25.4 cm)
New Zealand matai
Photo by artist

Hans Weissflog

WITH A ZEN-LIKE FOCUS, Hans Weissflog confidently applies his simple hand tools to spinning wood. His work reflects order and precision. Using only his eye to determine the shape, size, and spacing of each design element, Weissflog creates beautifully designed boxes and bowls, as well as intricate sculptural forms. His use of multiple-axis turning techniques always results in delicate but structurally strong designs. Because Weissflog thinks out the creation of a piece in advance, planning each component before he steps up to the lathe, his work bears no evidence of the minute variations usually present in handmade objects. A close examination of his symmetrical, beautifully proportioned pieces might lead the viewer to think they were produced by a machine. His boxes are legendary for their display of technical mastery and sense of design. His recent work contrasts the coarseness and irregularity of wood with precise designs and patterns.

◀ **Star Bowl** | 1999

2⅜ x 10½ inches
(6 x 26.7 cm)
Cocobolo

Photo by artist

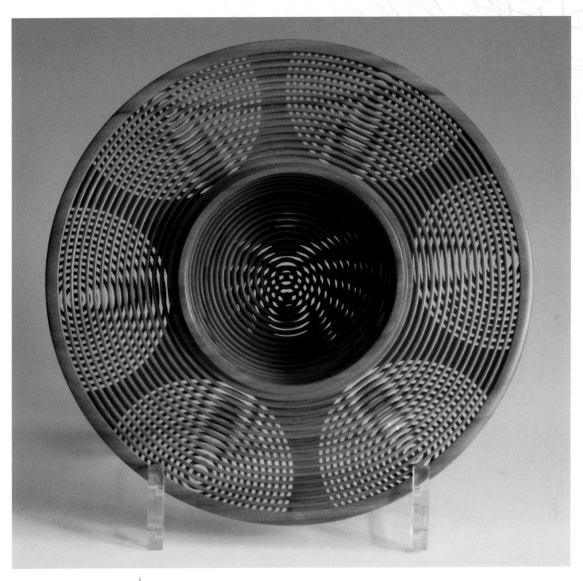

▲ **Saturn Star Bowl** | 2005

2¾ x 7 inches
(7 x 17.8 cm)
Putumuju

Photo by artist

▲ **Round Square Oval Box** | 1998

2 x 2 x 2 inches
(5.1 x 5.1 x 5.1 cm)
African blackwood, boxwood

Photo by artist

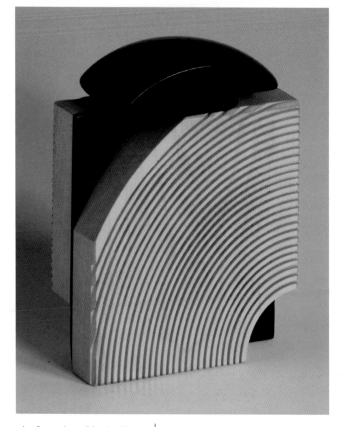

▲ **Quarter Circle Box** | 2002

2⅞ x 2⅜ x 1⅛ inches
(7.3 x 6 x 2.9 cm)
Boxwood, African blackwood

Photo by artist

" 'Klein und Fein' (German for 'small and fine') is my motto. "

▲ Square Disc Ball Box | 1999

2 x 3⅛ x 3⅛ inches
(5.1 x 7.9 x 7.9 cm)
African blackwood,
boxwood, maple

Photo by artist

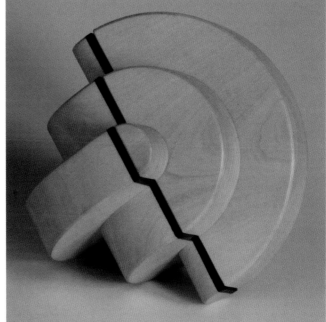

Drunken Box | 1994 ▶

3⅛ x 3⅛ x 3⅛ inches
(7.9 x 7.9 x 7.9 cm)
Boxwood, African blackwood

Photo by artist

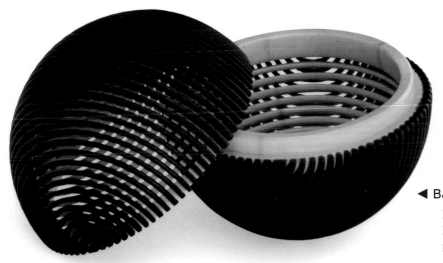

◀ **Ball Box, Turned Broken Through** │ 1991

Diameter, 2 inches (5.1 cm)
Boxwood, African blackwood
Photo by artist

Small Rocking Bowl │ 2004 ▶

2½ x 3⁵/₁₆ x 2½ inches
(6.4 x 8.4 x 6.4 cm)
Boxwood, African blackwood
Photo by artist

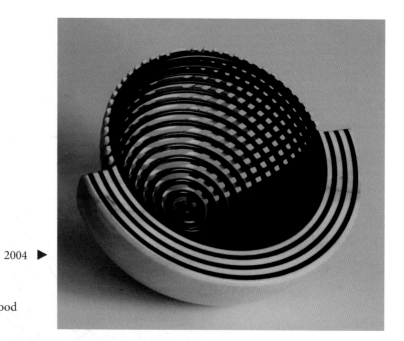

" I own more than 480 different kinds of wood. I love working with it because it's a living material. "

◀ **Saturn for D. Cortes** | 1992

1⁷/₁₆ x 3⅜ inches
(3.7 x 8.6 cm)
Boxwood
Photo by artist

▲ Boat Bowl | 2006

$3^{11}/_{16}$ x $6^{5}/_{8}$ x $5^{1}/_{8}$ inches
(9.4 x 16.8 x 13 cm)
Bocote
Photo by artist

" I try to create pieces where the observer can't take everything in with just one viewing. I want people to look at my work for a while and wonder if a piece might eventually work or if parts of it move. "

◄ **Second Drunken Box** | 2000
3⅛ x 3⅛ x 3⅛ inches
(7.9 x 7.9 x 7.9 cm)
Cocobolo
Photo by artist

◄ **Third Rocking Bowl** | 2007
3⁵/₁₆ x 7⁷/₁₆ x 5¼ inches
(8.4 x 18.9 x 13.3 cm)
Bocote
Photo by artist

Binh Pho

USING THE VESSEL AS A THREE-DIMENSIONAL CANVAS, Binh Pho covers his lathe-turned forms with precisely composed images that lead the viewer on a journey of discovery. Often, stylized elements such as dragonflies, cranes, and lotus blossoms are interspersed with swirling color fields and have a weightless, dream-like quality. These finely designed pieces are created through a complex process of sanding, airbrushing, and carving. Pho says that carving the form in order to create a design void or negative space is his favorite element of the work, because, for him, the negative space represents the unknown. Pho sometimes combines turned shapes to create complex forms that have a remarkable delicacy. His work is deeply personal, drawing on Oriental motifs and patterns that have a special resonance due to his Vietnamese heritage.

◄ **A Butterfly in the Dream** | 2005

21 x 8½ x 9 inches
(53.3 x 21.6 x 22.9 cm)
Box elder

Photo by artist

3½ x 2¾ x 2¾ inches
(8.9 x 7 x 7 cm)
Maple

Photo by artist

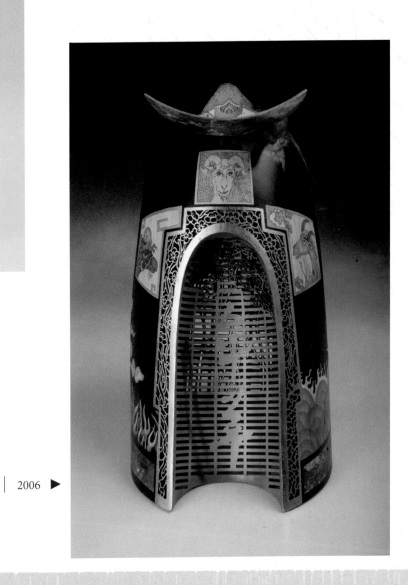

Three Goats in the Fairytale | 2006 ▶

12 x 8 x 7 inches
(30.5 x 20.3 x 17.8 cm)
Box elder, maple

Photo by artist

Waiting for the Moon to Go Away | 2006 ▼

31 x 15 x 9 inches
(78.7 x 38.1 x 22.9 cm)
Box elder, gingko

Photo by artist

▲ Au Revoir, Coquelicot | 2007

12 x 4½ x 4½ inches
(30.5 x 11.4 x 11.4 cm)
Box elder

Photo by artist

◀ **Rickshaw Park** │ 2006

13 x 8½ x 8½ inches
(33 x 21.6 x 21.6 cm)
Box elder

Photo by artist

" I put a soul into every piece

I create. I don't make objects;

I create characters. "

" I like to push the limits, using green wood and including the defective parts of wood in my designs in order to show the character of the material. "

▲ **Amor Renovatio** | 2006
16 x 9 x 9 inches
(40.6 x 22.9 x 22.9 cm)
Box elder
Photo by artist

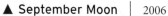

▲ **September Moon** | 2006
27 x 48 x 3½ inches
(68.6 x 121.9 x 8.9 cm)
Maple burl, maple, birch, Jacaranda
Photo by artist

9 x 6 x 6 inches
(22.9 x 15.2 x 15.2 cm)
Bradford pear

Photo by artist

BINH PHO

◀ **Red Moon** | 2007

7 x 3¾ x 3¾ inches
(17.8 x 9.5 x 9.5 cm)
Box elder
Photo by artist

" Over the years, I've made pieces to tell about
my past and my journey to the West—the chaos
of exodus in Southeast Asia, the escape from
communism to find freedom, the challenges and
rewards of my new life in America. "

◀ **Mystic Moon** | 2007

3 x 8 x 8 inches
(7.6 x 20.3 x 20.3 cm)
Box elder
Photo by artist

Destiny | 2007 ▶

14 x 9 x 9 inches
(35.6 x 22.9 x 22.9 cm)
Box elder

Photo by artist

Malcolm Tibbetts

THANKS TO ITS USE OF MULTIPLE, CONTRASTING WOODS, segmented turning allows for a high level of design and creativity. Malcolm Tibbetts makes the most of this process by creating pieces with complex patterns and color schemes. His intricately designed bowls, vases, and sculptural objects display incredible craftsmanship and ingenuity. Many of his pieces require innovative assembly solutions, much like puzzle solving. Tibbetts designs his pieces by drawing detailed blueprints using a CAD program on a computer. He has constructed individual pieces that contain up to 12,000 separate segments of wood. He works with a variety of domestic and exotic woods from around the world and does not use stains, paints, or dyes. Richly patterned and ingeniously constructed, his pieces feel modern and artful while exhibiting strong ties to nature.

◀ **Bourbon Street Blues** | 2006

29 x 11 inches
(73.7 x 27.9 cm)
Curly maple, Gabon ebony

Photo by artist

▲ Black-and-White Teapot | 2004

5 x 8 inches
(12.7 x 20.3 cm)
Holly, Gabon ebony

Photo by artist

◀ **Fortitude** | 2007

12 x 7 inches
(30.5 x 17.8 cm)
Banksia pod,
Macassar ebony

Photo by artist

" There are few art forms that offer as much freedom as segmented woodturning. By combining components, I can create just about any shape. "

Gabriel's Dilemma | 2006 ▶

Height, 18 inches
(45.7 cm)
Kingwood,
Brazilian tulipwood,
Gabon ebony

Photo by artist

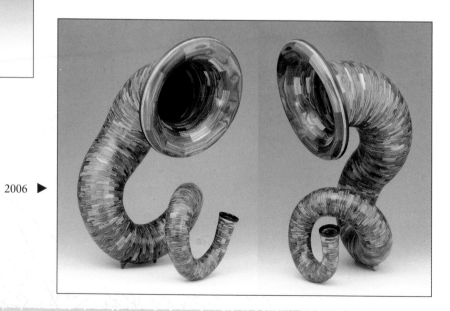

◀ **Galactic Journey** | 2007

22 x 22 x 22 inches
(55.9 x 55.9 x 55.9 cm)
Various exotic woods

Photo by artist

◄ Rocky Road Ahead | 2006

20 x 9 x 9 inches
(50.8 x 22.9 x 22.9 cm)
Curly maple, holly,
various exotic woods

Photo by artist

Celebration | 2005 ►

17 x 12 inches
(43.2 x 30.5 cm)
Myrtlewood,
canarywood, ebony

Photo by artist

▲ Men in the Shadows | 2007

14 x 8 inches
(35.6 x 20.3 cm)
Curly maple, Texas ebony,
Gabon ebony

Photo by artist

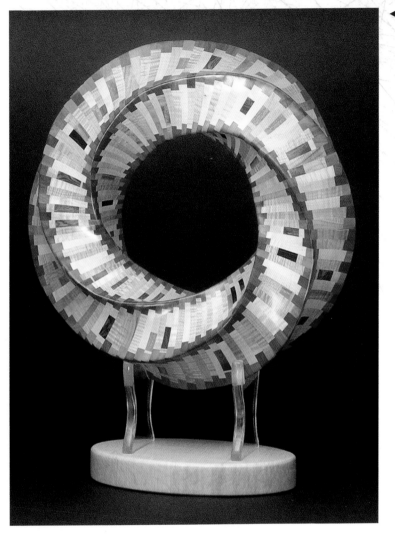

◀ Unity │ 2005
25 x 6 inches
(63.5 x 15.2 cm)
Various exotic woods
Photo by artist

" I can spend weeks trying to solve a particularly
difficult construction puzzle. The joy of discovering
unconventional solutions drives me to succeed. "

MALCOLM TIBBETTS

◄ **Mobius Sonata** | 2005

15 x 20 x 10 inches
(38.1 x 50.8 x 25.4 cm)
Bird's-eye maple, Gabon ebony

Photo by artist

Tolerance | 2006 ►

32 x 20 x 8 inches
(81.3 x 50.8 x 20.3 cm)
Myrtlewood,
Macassar ebony

Photos by artist

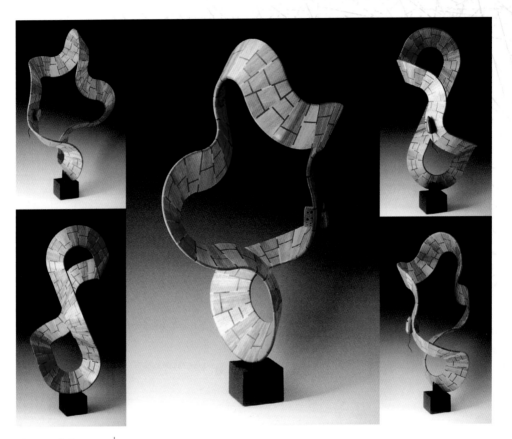

▲ **Persistence** | 2005

29 x 13 x 13 inches
(73.7 x 33 x 33 cm)
Lyptus, purpleheart
Photos by artist

" There are three elements of segmented woodturning that can't be ignored: form, precise joinery, and consistent wood grain alignment. Without adherence to all three of these elements, I've found that success is unlikely. "

Alain Mailland

INSPIRED BY THE FORMS AND EXPRESSIONS OF NATURAL ELEMENTS, Alain Mailland has developed his own wonderfully innovative, slightly surreal style of wooden sculpture. Mailland refers to his whimsical turned and carved forms as "hybrid vegetable, animal, or cosmic creatures"—a fitting description for the formally inventive sculptures he makes from wet, green wood. Reminiscent of marine life, these cleanly designed pieces have a singular organic symmetry. They're neither plant nor animal, yet they possess qualities of both. For Mailland, such combinations symbolize the harmony that exists in nature. Other sculptures are inspired by flower shapes. Mailland carves these blossoming forms by hand with special curved tools. He has developed his own technique for hollowing, and his expertise allows him to produce pieces with long, beautiful lines and logical design structures.

◀ **Touch of Zen** | 2000
9¹³/₁₆ x 7⅞ inches
(25 x 20 cm)
Locust burl
Photo by artist

Eurêka | 2003 ▶
19¹¹/₁₆ x 21⅝ inches
(50 x 55 cm)
Hackberry
Photo by artist

◀ **Plankton Dream** | 2006

8¼ x 3¹⁵/₁₆ inches
(21 x 10 cm)
Heather root
Photo by artist

" Whenever I turn a piece, I feel that I'm reproducing the secret rules of the universe, because everything in it turns, from atoms to galaxies. "

Babel | 2000 ▶

7¹/₁₆ x 7⅞ inches
(18 x 20 cm)
Heather root
Photo by artist

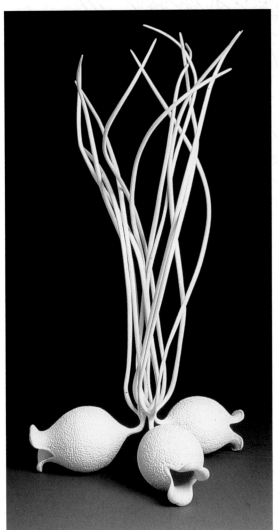

◄ **The Soul Sisters** | 1998

Height, 13¾ inches
(35 cm)
Hackberry

Photo by artist

Blob | 2001 ►

13¾ x 5⅞ inches
(35 x 15 cm)
Juniper burl

Photo by artist

18⅞ x 25³/₁₆ inches
(48 x 64 cm)
Cherry burl

Photo by artist

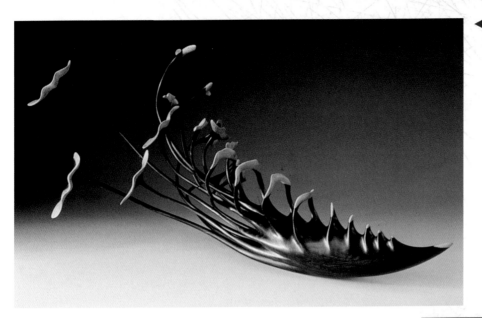

◀ **The Guide** | 2004

15⁵/₁₆ x 9¹/₁₆ inches
(39 x 23 cm)
African blackwood

Photo by artist

" Woodturning is a dreaming process,
like a meditation, and the result is
the incarnation of the dream. "

Dancing Pelagie | 2005 ▶

13 ¾ x 15 ¹¹/₁₆ inches
(35 x 40 cm)
Pistachio

Photo by artist

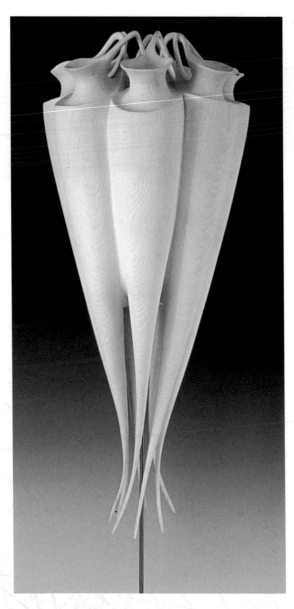

◀ Seven Wise Men Dancing | 2006

9^{13}/$_{16}$ x 20^{13}/$_{16}$ inches
(25 x 53 cm)
Hackberry
Photo by artist

" I live in the south of France, where the landscape is covered with boxwood, pistachio, and heather trees that suffer from the heat during the summer. These trees develop incredible roots with figured burls. The roots are real wonders, and they're my main resource for wood. "

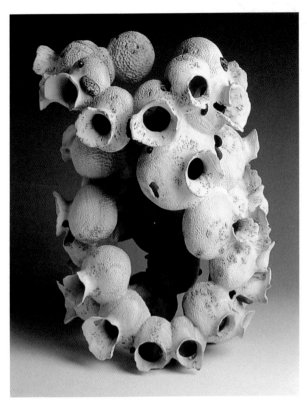

◀ **The Stone Eater** | 2000

9¹³/₁₆ x 17¹¹/₁₆ inches
(25 x 45 cm)
Elm burl

Photo by artist

Mother Fish and Her Babies | 1999 ▶

11¹³/₁₆ x 5⅞ inches
(30 x 15 cm)
Locust burl

Photo by artist

Clay Foster

LIKE ANCIENT ARTIFACTS DISCOVERED IN A CAVE, Clay Foster's pots and bowls have a mysterious primal quality. Drawing inspiration from a variety of channels—the history and architecture of the Southwest; religious totems that have an aura of sacredness; everyday objects that become infused with a special significance over time—Foster produces pieces that are artless yet sophisticated. He savors the imperfections found in wood, using them as an added source of texture. He favors embellishments like beads, paint, and wire—elements that give his pieces an extra earthiness. The rough-hewn wooden tables and columns he uses as pedestals for his pieces add another dimension to his work. Foster leaves their distressed surfaces untouched, preferring naturally flawed exteriors to finished ones. This impeccable attention to detail is central to his creative vision about what will make a work whole and complete.

◀ **White Diamonds** | 2006

Height, 17 inches
(43.2 cm)
Palo bianco

Photo by artist

▲ **Vessel with Fine Line Pattern** | 1996

11 x 8 inches
(27.9 x 20.3 cm)
Unidentified species

Photo by artist

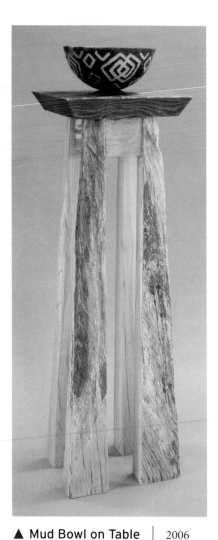

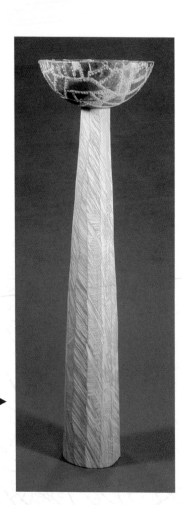

◄ Temple Bowl on 5 Vigas Tower | 2006

45 x 11 x 11 inches
(114.3 x 27.9 x 27.9 cm)
Unidentified species

Photo by artist

▲ Mud Bowl on Table | 2006

Height, 51 inches
(129.5 cm)
Unidentified species

Photo by artist

Precious Metal | 2006 ►

45 x 11 inches
(114.3 x 27.9 cm)
Spalted pink ivory burl,
yellow pine

Photo by artist

◀ Hueco Font | 2003

33 x 10 x 10 inches
(83.8 x 25.4 x 25.4 cm)
Unidentified species
Photo by artist

" Life is not clean, direct, and predictable. It's messy.
It serpentines. It's interrupted by cracks and voids.
My work reflects this unpredictability. "

" As I work, I find that the resolution of a problem can often result in a wonderful shift into a new pattern. But sometimes there are problems that can't be resolved, only endured. "

▲ **Vessel with Green and Yellow Pattern** | 1995

13 x 6 inches
(33 x 15.2 cm)
Unidentified species
Photo by artist

Vessel with Wild Goose Chase Pattern | 1994 ▶

17 x 6 inches (43.2 x 15.2 cm)
Unidentified species
Photo by artist

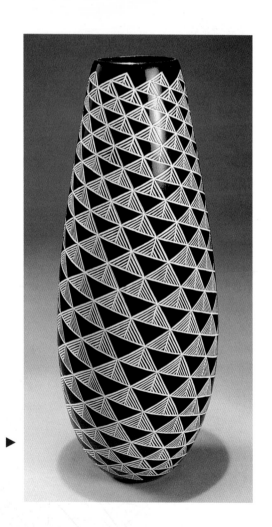

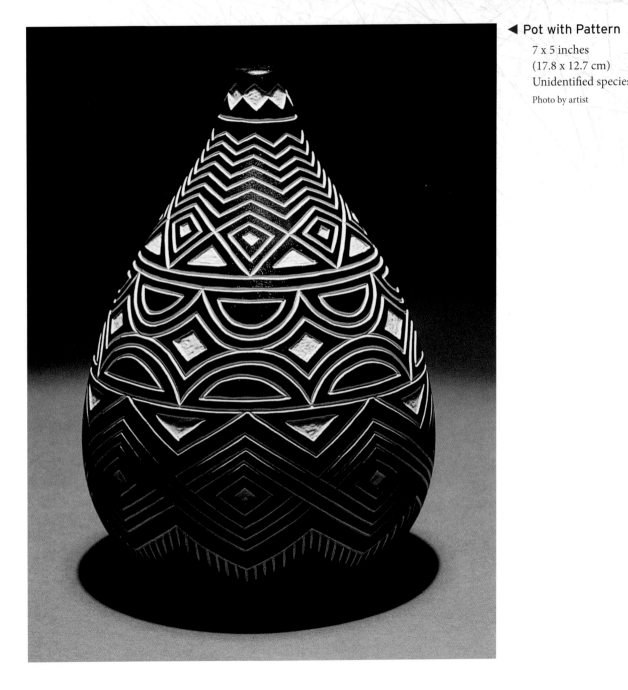

CLAY FOSTER

You Call My Name | 1999 ▶

57 x 17 x 11 inches
(144.8 x 43.2 x 27.9 cm)
Oak
Photo by artist

Mud Pot | 2000 ▶

16 x 8 inches
(40.6 x 20.3 cm)
Oak
Photo by artist

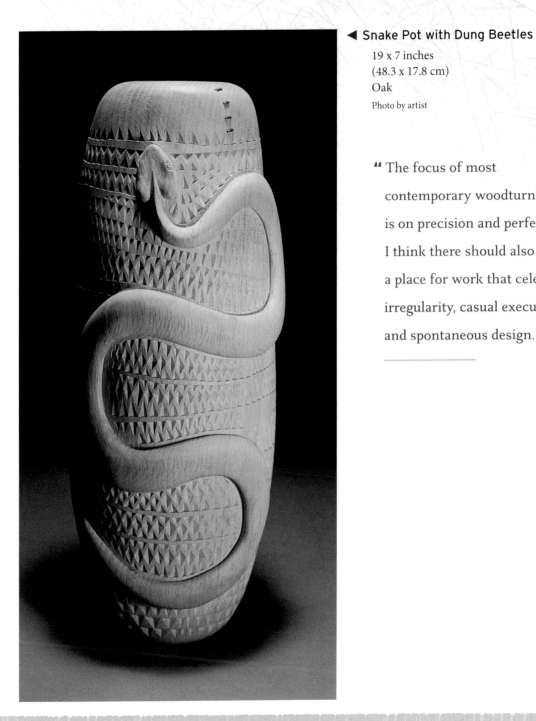

◀ **Snake Pot with Dung Beetles** | 1999

19 x 7 inches
(48.3 x 17.8 cm)
Oak
Photo by artist

" The focus of most
contemporary woodturning
is on precision and perfection.
I think there should also be
a place for work that celebrates
irregularity, casual execution,
and spontaneous design. "

CLAY FOSTER

Gerrit Van Ness

CHARACTERIZED BY VIVID COLORS, clever composition, and an offbeat sensibility, the work of Gerrit Van Ness pushes boundaries. Narrative sculpture is how he describes his dioramas and mixed media pieces—expertly designed forms that employ a variety of materials besides wood. Van Ness often uses elements like metal, newspaper, and sand to create sculptural still lifes that are at once surreal, edgy, and sophisticated. An accomplished craftsman with a wide range of skills, he has the ability to make a turned wooden piece look like a real object. His wooden paint cans, for example, could easily be mistaken for the real thing. Van Ness' out-of-the ordinary creations are designed to raise questions and to poke fun at stereotypes and current issues in our society. Look at one of his detailed pieces up close, and a question immediately comes to mind: How did he do that?

Bad Teapot, Queenie, Bubba | 2002 ▼

Each, 6 x 8 x 4 inches
(15.2 x 20.3 x 10.2 cm)
Various

Photo by Chuck Finn

▲ Can-A-Copia | 2003

4½ x 13½ x 6½ inches
(11.4 x 34.3 x 16.5 cm)
Various

Photo by Chuck Finn

◀ Baghdad Taxi | 2006

14½ x 18 x 12 inches
(36.8 x 45.7 x 30.5 cm)
Maple, poplar

Photo by William Alan

Sunny-Side Up | 2006 ▶

9½ x 18½ x 11 inches
(24.1 x 47 x 27.9 cm)
Poplar, maple

Photo by William Alan

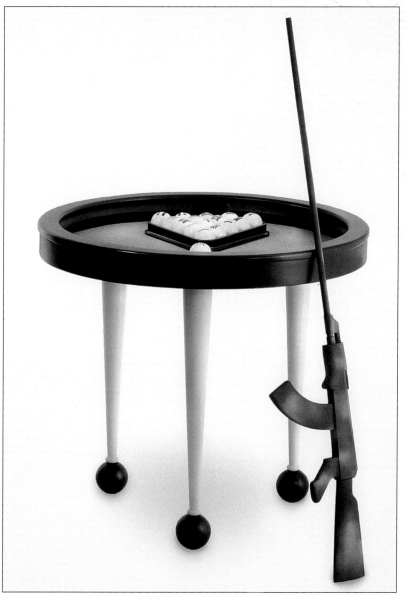

52 x 36 x 36 inches
(132.1 x 91.4 x 91.4 cm)
Poplar, maple

Photos by William Alan

" One challenge for me is to create complex pieces that appear to be simple. "

Liar, Liar | 2007 ▶

19 x 48 x 18 inches
(48.3 x 121.9 x 45.7 cm)
Maple, poplar

Photo by William Alan

" I know a piece has hit its mark

when viewers attribute beliefs to me

that they're really finding within themselves. "

◀ **Sudden Impact** | 2002

4½ x 12½ x 8 inches
(11.4 x 31.8 x 20.3 cm)
Maple, poplar

Photo by Chuck Finn

▲ **Envy** | 2007

11½ x 23 x 14½ inches
(29.2 x 58.4 x 36.8 cm)
Poplar, maple

Photo by William Alan

◀ **Feelin' Good!** | 2006
21 x 10 x 5½ inches
(53.3 x 25.4 x 14 cm)
Maple, poplar
Photo by William Alan

" I normally have at least six pieces in progress at any given time. I typically do a small thumbnail sketch as a reminder for a certain idea, then jump into creating the piece when the mood hits me. "

Funnel of Love | 2003 ▶
21½ x 17 x 12 inches
(54.6 x 43.2 x 30.5 cm)
Maple, poplar
Photo by Chuck Finn

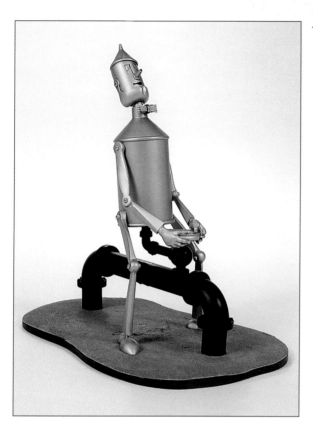

◀ **Ride 'Em Cowboy!** │ 2005

16½ x 16 x 11 inches
(41.9 x 40.6 x 27.9 cm)
Maple

Photo by Chuck Finn

End of the Road │ 2007 ▶

16 x 25 x 16 inches
(40.6 x 63.5 x 40.6 cm)
Maple, poplar

Photo by William Alan

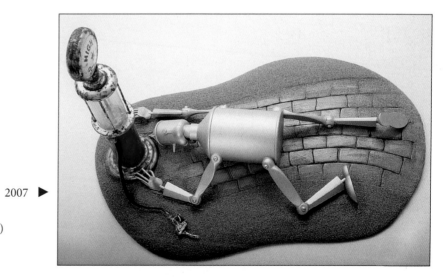

Christian Burchard

THROUGH HIS CREATIVE USE OF THE LATHE, Christian Burchard shows us that the tool is much more than just a machine used for making round pieces of wood. Subtle elements like strategically placed grooves add balance and unity to his turned pieces. Burchard's work pays homage to the natural surfaces and flaws that characterize wood. If he adds any decorative elements to his pieces, they're spare and logical. Some of Burchard's pieces are made from fresh-cut Madrone wood that was allowed to warp as it dried. These works feature surfaces that mimic the natural flow of the wood grain, with only a faint suggestion of embellishment. Finely crafted yet free of artifice, Burchard's work demonstrates the advantages of designing with the essence of the wood in mind. Letting the material speak for itself, he exposes the wood's inner beauty—always to its best advantage.

◀ Spherical Vessels | 2001
Largest, 12 inches
(30.5 cm) in diameter
Madrone burl
Photo by Rob Jaffe

▲ **Black Baskets** │ 2000

Largest, 12 inches
(30.5 cm) in diameter
Madrone burl

Photo by Rob Jaffe

Running with the Bulls | 2002 ▶

18 x 5 x 18 inches
(45.7 x 12.7 x 45.7 cm)
Madrone burl

Photo by Rob Jaffe

" My work is about my relationship with
nature, my desire to connect with it on a deep
level. Trying to get under its skin. Being part
of it. Searching, finding something sacred,
adding my touch, wrestling with it. "

Jason | 2000 ▶

18 x 12 x 4 inches
(45.7 x 30.5 x 10.2 cm)
Dogwood burl,
rosewood

Photo by Rob Jaffe

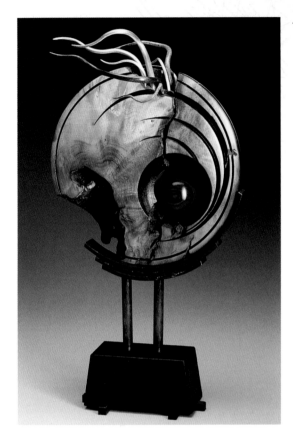

◀ **Medusa** │ 2000

22 x 12 x 8 inches
(55.9 x 30.5 x 20.3 cm)
Dogwood burl, rosewood

Photo by Rob Jaffe

Looking at Yesterday │ 1998 ▶

34 x 18 x 6 inches
(86.4 x 45.7 x 15.2 cm)
Maple burl

Photo by Rob Jaffe

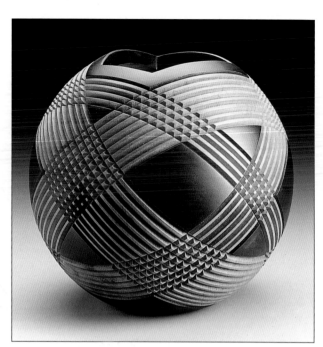

◀ **Spherical Vessel, Old Earth Series** │ 1996

Diameter, 12 inches
(30.5 cm)
California bay laurel
Photo by Rob Jaffe

" To work this closely with nature is a blessing, but
it's often overwhelming. Sometimes I wonder,
'What is needed here of me? How can I match
the beauty of this living thing?' "

Stepping Lightly, Old Earth Series │ 1995 ▶

Diameter, 7 inches
(17.8 cm)
Cuban mahogany
Photo by Rob Jaffe

◀ **Baskets** | 1999

16 x 1 inches
(40.6 x 2.5 cm)
Madrone burl

Photo by Rob Jaffe

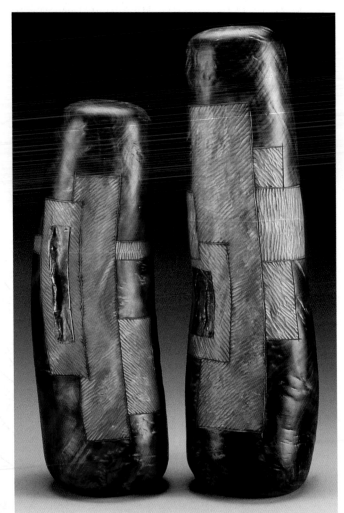

◀ **The Chroniclers** | 2003

Tallest, 22 x 6 inches
(55.9 x 15.2 cm)
Madrone burl

Photo by Rob Jaffe

▼ **Ziggurat** | 1993

14 x 8 inches
(35.6 x 20.3 cm)
Madrone root

Photo by Rob Jaffe

▲ **Untitled** | 2005

Largest, 12 x 3 inches
(30.5 x 7.6 cm)
Madrone root

Photo by Rob Jaffe

" By working with wet wood that has a high water content and by cutting or turning my forms very thin, I take advantage of the changes that occur as the wood dries. Very dynamic changes often take place. "

Hugh McKay

CHARACTERIZED BY COMPLEX SURFACE FINISHES, the work of Hugh McKay is at once delicate and bold. Texture is an important part of his creative process, and McKay uses it in ways that seem natural and logical. His inspired, original interpretations of vessels help us to see these traditional forms from a new perspective. McKay, who owns a glass-casting foundry, frequently adds glass to his pieces in order to create visual and tactile interest. He also uses metal in his work, an addition that sets up provocative contrasts between design materials. His wooden sculptures often have an elemental quality. The work of an artist in command of his craft, McKay's carved pieces are unrestrained yet perfectly controlled. Thanks to his technical prowess, he gives us work that is powerful, daring, and possessed of a wonderful lyrical virtuosity.

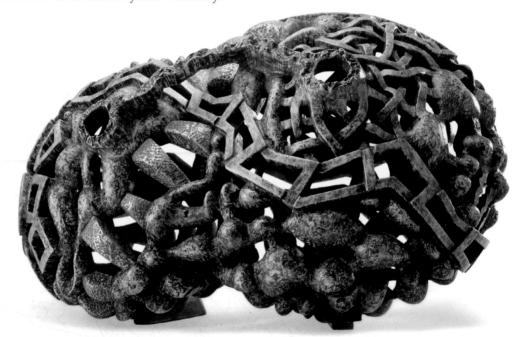

Irta | 2004 ▶
16 x 22 x 12 inches
(40.6 x 55.9 x 30.5 cm)
Maple burl
Photo by artist

Yes | 1995 ▶

24 x 13 x 13 inches
(61 x 33 x 33 cm)
Fiddleback maple

Photo by artist

Untitled | 1996 ▶

4 x 11 x 11 inches
(10.2 x 27.9 x 27.9 cm)
Myrtle

Photo by artist

◀ **Ruuach** | 1998

14 x 18 x 18 inches
(35.6 x 45.7 x 45.7 cm)
Madrone burl

Photo by artist

" I love the coastline—a place where two separate worlds meet and come together in the most interesting ways. I try to combine different materials in the same fashion. "

▲ Opris | 2001

8 x 10 x 10 inches
(20.3 x 25.4 x 25.4 cm)
Maple burl, alabaster

Photo by artist

Untitled | 1997 ▶

9 x 12 x 12 inches
(22.9 x 30.5 x 30.5 cm)
Madrone burl, translucent orange alabaster

Photo by artist

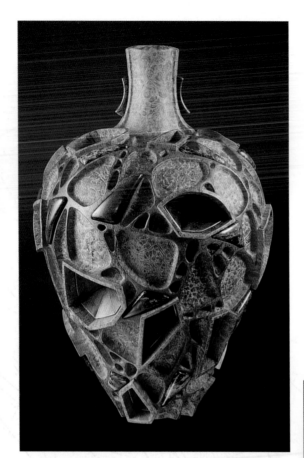

"To me, some of the most interesting and intense sculpture is found in contemporary jewelry. I try to emulate that visual intensity in my work. "

▲ Aeon | 1993

21 x 14 x 14 inches
(53.3 x 35.6 x 35.6 cm)
Madrone burl
Photo by artist

Myakandra | 1996 ▶

15 x 25 x 25 inches
(38.1 x 63.5 x 63.5 cm)
Maple burl
Photo by artist

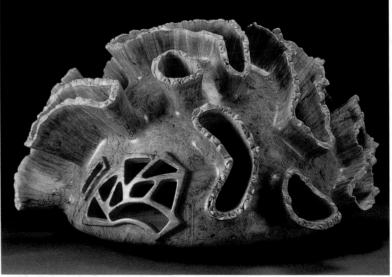

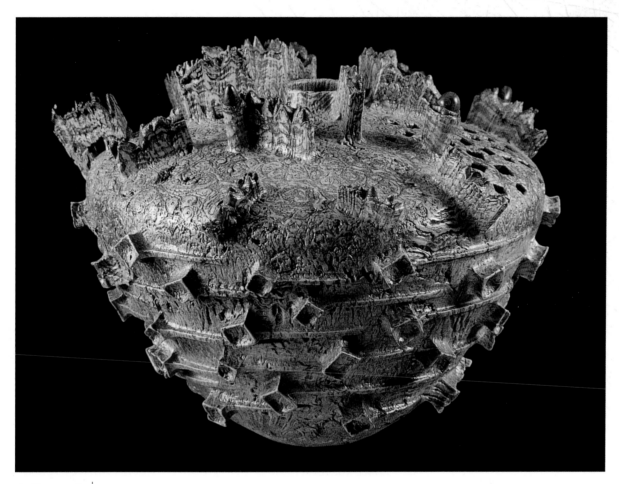

▲ **Squared** | 1994

14 x 15 x 15 inches
(35.6 x 38.1 x 38.1 cm)
Maple burl

Photo by artist

Pentapot #2 | 1996 ▶

16 x 18 x 15 inches
(40.6 x 45.7 x 38.1 cm)
Madrone burl

Photo by artist

◀ **Melisma** | 1997

18 x 18 x 8½ inches
(45.7 x 45.7 x 21.6 cm)
Quilted maple

Photo by artist

" Landscapes are a great source for new ideas to express in sculpture. I also love rock formations. My mind literally trips over itself with fresh insights into how matter can be formed when I get around the right 'rockpile.' "

▲ **T-Pot #20** | 1996

11 x 11 x 7 inches
(27.9 x 27.9 x 17.8 cm)
Maple burl

Photo by artist

Marilyn Campbell

TREATING WOOD AS A CANVAS FOR EXPRESSING HER IDEAS, Marilyn Campbell produces forms that are remarkably fluid and refined. Unlike many woodturners, she doesn't highlight her material's natural characteristics. Instead, she emphasizes design for its own sake, creating sculptural objects that have a unique aesthetic purity. Campbell cuts, colors, pierces, and reassembles her lathe-based forms so that the individual parts work in harmony together. Characterized by bold lines and an elegant black-and-white color scheme, many of her recent pieces were inspired by vintage and contemporary handbags. These pieces are design-oriented and, as Campbell puts it, "influenced by the look of culture, rather than of nature." Manipulating texture, line, and contrast to create artful compositions, Campbell creates work that is truly ground-breaking.

Origins | 2003 ▶
9½ x 8 inches
(24.1 x 20.3 cm)
Walnut
Photo by artist

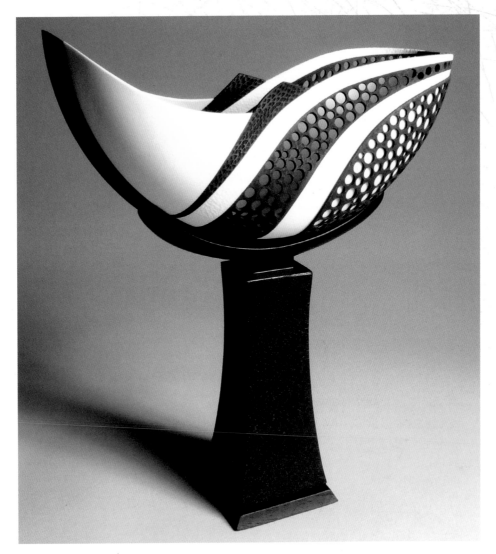

▲ **Veiled Lady** | 2007

9 x 8 x 2½ inches
(22.9 x 20.3 x 6.4 cm)
Holly, cherry, purpleheart

Photo by artist

Black Tie Affair | 2005 ▶

7½ x 10 x 3 inches
(19.1 x 25.4 x 7.6 cm)
Holly, walnut, ebony

Photo by artist

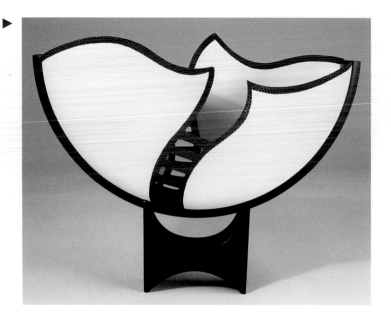

" I remember saying many years
ago that I myself didn't want to be
'in the picture.' How wrong I was.
When I have created a piece,
it's a part of me that I send
out into the world. "

◀ I Have A Feeling We're Not in Kansas Anymore | 2005

10 x 9½ inches
(25.4 x 24.1 cm)
Holly, walnut

Photo by artist

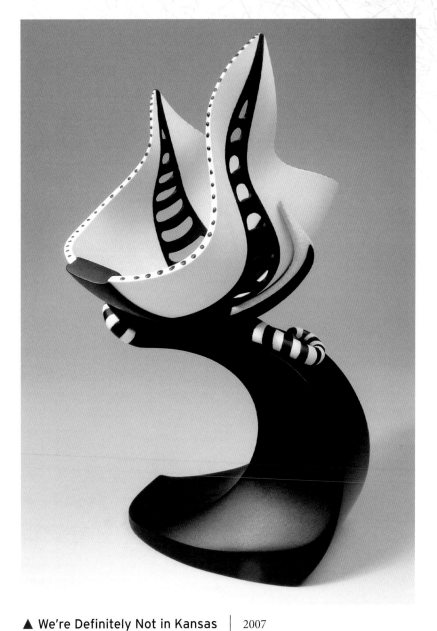

▲ **We're Definitely Not in Kansas** | 2007

    9 x 5½ inches
    (22.9 x 14 cm)
    Holly, cherry, walnut
    Photo by artist

" I love to see a piece of work take shape and watch its 'personality' appear. To me, each piece has its own individual character. "

Pop the Cork | 2007 ▶
9 x 8 x 2½ inches
(22.9 x 20.3 x 6.4 cm)
Holly, maple, purpleheart
Photo by artist

◀ **Explorer's Club** | 2007
7 x 9 x 3 inches
(17.8 x 22.9 x 7.6 cm)
Holly, ebony
Photo by artist

▲ **Last Waltz** | 2007

7¾ x 9 x 2½ inches
(19.7 x 22.9 x 6.4 cm)
Holly, curly maple, purpleheart

Photo by artist

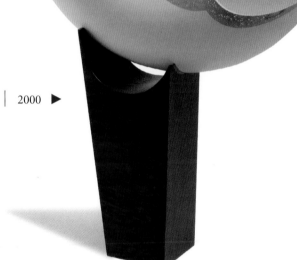

" The excitement of making a piece keeps me involved and focused. New ideas, the challenge of creating work that evokes a response, and the people I meet along the way are all fuel for my enthusiasm. "

Bloomin' Purple | 2000 ▶

10 x 9 inches
(25.4 x 22.9 cm)
Holly, purpleheart
Photo by artist

◀ **Rare Elements** | 1999

10 x 12 x 2 inches
(25.4 x 30.5 x 5.1 cm)
Holly, ebony
Photo by artist

Huron | 2001 ▶

10 x 10 x 2½ inches
(25.4 x 25.4 x 6.4 cm)
Holly, walnut

Photo by artist

◀ **Snow Home** | 2000

7½ x 12½ x 7 inches
(19.1 x 31.8 x 17.8 cm)
Holly, walnut

Photo by artist

Stephen Hatcher

COMBINING THE TECHNIQUES OF WOODTURNING AND STONE CARVING, Stephen Hatcher has produced a body of work that is remarkable for its level of detail. His pieces are made from highly figured woods and transparent crystals that are accentuated with dyes and polished to a high sheen. Inspired by the changing of the seasons, his vessels and platters often feature precisely composed landscapes and nature scenes. His designs are hand-carved, and the surface of his work—glossy and mirror-like—enhances the stone inlay and the natural grain patterns of the wood. Hatcher, who has an interest in Japanese art and Buddhist poetry, infuses his work with serenity and harmony. Many of his lidded vessels are topped by graceful finials inspired by Torii gates seen in Japanese gardens. Like oriental silk paintings, his compositions are wonderfully complex and offer something new with each viewing.

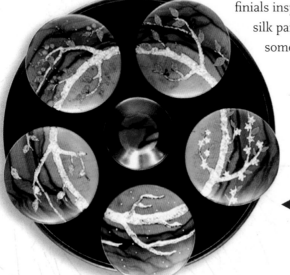

◀ **Seasons of the Orient** | 2003

4 x 8 x 8 inches
(10.2 x 20.3 x 20.3 cm)
Macassar ebony,
Asian striped ebony

Photo by artist

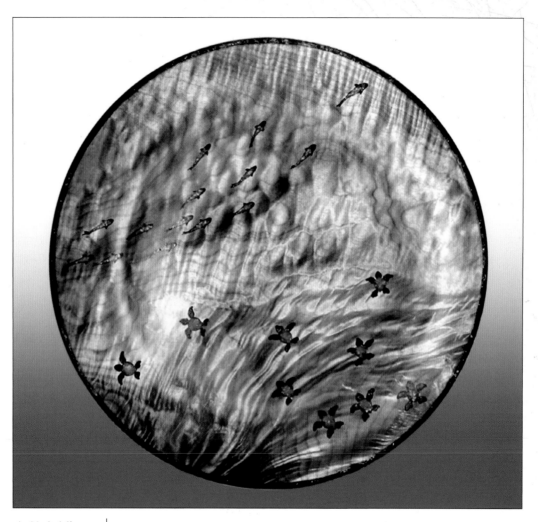

▲ **Hatchlings** | 2004

14 x 14 x 2 inches
(35.6 x 35.6 x 5.1 cm)
Bigleaf maple

Photo by artist

" In each piece that I create, the primary influence comes from the wood itself. "

▲ **Untitled** | 2005

7 x 4 x 4 inches
(17.8 x 10.2 x 10.2 cm)
Bigleaf maple
Photo by artist

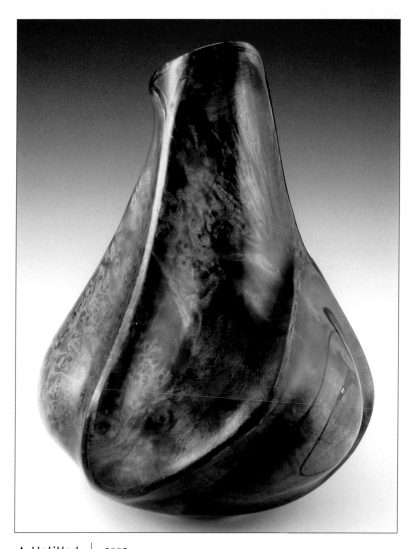

▲ **Untitled** | 2005

7 x 4 x 4 inches
(17.8 x 10.2 x 10.2 cm)
Bigleaf maple
Photo by artist

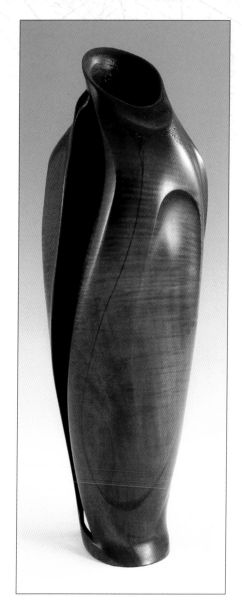

▲ **The Shroud** | 2005

11½ x 4 x 4 inches
(29.2 x 10.2 x 10.2 cm)
Bigleaf maple
Photo by artist

◀ **Translucence #3** | 2007

7½ x 13 x 5 inches
(19.1 x 33 x 12.7 cm)
Bigleaf maple, koa,
Indian ebony

Photo by artist

A Plum Blossom Falls | 2007 ▶

4¼ x 5¾ x 5¾ inches
(10.8 x 14.6 x 14.6 cm)
Bigleaf maple, Indian ebony

Photo by artist

▲ Beneath the Shadows of Leaves | 2006

16 x 6¾ x 6¾ inches
(40.6 x 17.1 x 17.1 cm)
Bigleaf maple, Brazilian rosewood

Photo by artist

▲ Autumn Wind | 2007

4¾ x 5¼ x 5¼ inches
(12.1 x 13.3 x 13.3 cm)
Bigleaf maple, Indian ebony

Photo by artist

" In my work I use the flora and fauna of the four seasons as a metaphor for the transience of beauty and the adversity of life. "

◀ **Daimyo II** | 2007

10¼ x 5½ x 3¼ inches
(26 x 14 x 8.3 cm)
Macassar ebony, bigleaf maple,
Indian ebony

Photo by artist

▼ **Winter Cranes** | 2007

20 x 20 x 2 inches
(50.8 x 50.8 x 5.1 cm)
Bigleaf maple

Photo by artist

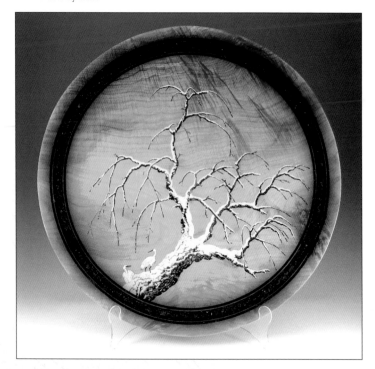

▲ Weeping Cherry | 2007

13¾ x 6½ x 6½ inches
(34.9 x 16.5 x 16.5 cm)
Bigleaf maple, African blackwood
Photo by artist

" I use local bigleaf maple in most of my pieces because it has dramatic figure. Figure drives the imagery I inlay and becomes a part of that imagery. **"**

John Jordan

THE SIMPLE BUT FINELY DETAILED VESSELS made by John Jordan are models of quiet craftsmanship. Engaging the viewer's natural reverence for gorgeous wood and harmonious design, his beautifully wrought pieces are pure in form and rich in detail. Jordan textures and carves his pieces to create visual and tactile contrasts. He creates vessels in a range of shapes. His bottle forms, lidded jars, and tall vessels may be bleached or dyed. In order to downplay wood grain and concentrate on form, he paints some of his pieces black. Appropriately enough, when he discusses his work, Jordan uses terms that could apply to any artistic medium. "My pieces are about pattern, texture, contrast and movement," he says. In Jordan's work, all of these elements work together beautifully—and without compromise.

Red Maple Vessel | 2003 ▶
16 x 12 x 12 inches
(40.6 x 30.5 x 30.5 cm)
Red maple
Photo by artist

▲ **Red Maple Burl Vessel** | 2001

10 x 11 x 11 inches
(25.4 x 27.9 x 27.9 cm)
Red maple burl

Photo by artist

◀ **Black Trio** | 1991

Tallest, 14 x 8 x 8 inches
(35.6 x 20.3 x 20.3 cm)
Maple

Photo by John S. Cummings

" There's no wood
stored in my studio
at all, so it's a bright,
clean space. I've found
that this has a very
positive impact on my
work and on my state
of mind. "

◀ Black Vessel | 1995

11 x 10 x 10 inches
(27.9 x 25.4 x 25.4 cm)
Maple

Photo by John S. Cummings

Box Elder Vessel | 1993 ▶

11 x 8 x 8 inches
(27.9 x 20.3 x 20.3 cm)
Box elder

Photos by John S. Cummings

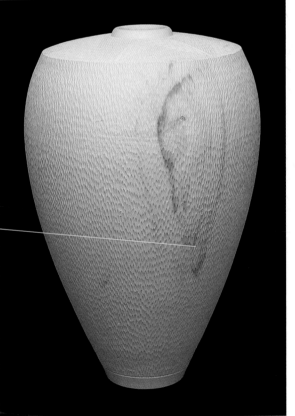

◀ **English Walnut Vessel** | 2002

4 x 6 x 6 inches
(10.2 x 15.2 x 15.2 cm)
English walnut

Photo by artist

▲ **Cherry Vessel** | 2006

10 x 12 x 12 inches
(25.4 x 30.5 x 30.5 cm)
Cherry

Photo by artist

◀ **Walnut Vessel** | 2006

10 x 10 x 10 inches
(25.4 x 25.4 x 25.4 cm)
Walnut

Photo by artist

" The intangible quality that the piece is 'right' that comes with putting emotion and feeling into the work is, for me, most important. "

◀ **Tall Jar** | 2002

17 x 10 x 10 inches
(43.2 x 25.4 x 25.4 cm)
Red maple burl

Photo by artist

> " Many of the woods that I use are from the dump or from construction sites. I find great satisfaction in creating elegant objects from material that was destined to be buried or burned. "

▲ **Box Elder Jar** | 1997
   12 x 9 x 9 inches
   (30.5 x 22.9 x 22.9 cm)
   Box elder
   Photo by artist

▲ **Box Elder Vessel** | 2000
   8 x 11 x 11 inches
   (20.3 x 27.9 x 27.9 cm)
   Box elder
   Photo by artist

◄ **Box Elder Bottle** | 1989

12 x 9 x 9 inches
(30.5 x 22.9 x 22.9 cm)
Box elder

Photo by John S. Cummings

Michael Hosaluk

THE QUESTION OF HOW SURFACE RELATES TO FORM is one that Michael Hosaluk returns to again and again in his work. He approaches his art with the eye of an innovator. Tapping into a range of moods, from surreal to humorous to classic, he has produced a diverse body of work that includes clean, streamlined vessels, functional yet playful teapots and candlesticks, and abstract sculptural objects. Working to establish juxtapositions that involve texture, color, and shape, Hosaluk mines the relationships between design elements in his pieces. He also sets up challenges for himself as he creates, playing with balance when he assembles a work or experimenting with the interaction that can occur between groups of pieces. Demonstrating boldness of vision and technical mastery, Hosaluk's work is at once contemporary and timeless—at home in the art world of today but tied firmly to the woodturning traditions of the past.

◄ **Container** | 2002

16 x 4 x 6 inches
(40.6 x 10.2 x 15.2 cm)
Maple

Photo by AK Photos

▲ **Containers** | 2002

    6 x 14 x 10 inches
    (15.2 x 35.6 x 25.4 cm)
    Maple

    Photo by AK Photos

▲ **Candlesticks** | 2004

11 x 16 x 4 inches
(27.9 x 40.6 x 10.2 cm)
Maple
Photo by AK Photos

" Every so often, I challenge myself to make beautiful, simple vessels that fit in the palm of the hand and have all the hallmarks of what I see as the most important elements of object making. "

▼ **Little Black Bowls** | 2003

   6 x 12 x 6 inches
   (15.2 x 30.5 x 15.2 cm)
   Arbutus
   Photo by AK Photos

▲ **Bird Vase** | 2007

   11 x 4 x 4 inches
   (27.9 x 10.2 x 10.2 cm)
   Maple
   Photo by AK Photos

◀ **Metamorphosis** │ 2005

13 x 24 x 5 inches
(33 x 61 x 12.7 cm)
Arbutus
Photo by AK Photos

Containers │ 2003 ▶

10 x 12 x 8 inches
(25.4 x 30.5 x 20.3 cm)
Jarrah, maple
Photo by AK Photos

" In my pieces, I am constantly
visiting the concept of
relationships, not only of male-
female relationships, but of how
forms reflect concepts and ideas. "

◀ **Codependence** | 2005

14 x 10 x 5 inches
(35.6 x 25.4 x 12.7 cm)
Arbutus

Photo by AK Photos

MICHAEL **HOSALUK**

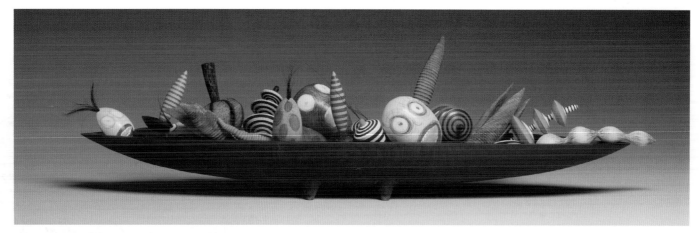

◀ **Scribble #2** │ 2006

14 x 6 x 6 inches
(35.6 x 15.2 x 15.2 cm)
Maple

Photo by AK Photos

▲ **Bowl of Strange Fruit** │ 2007

6 x 22 x 5 inches
(15.2 x 55.9 x 12.7 cm)
Maple, birch, arbutus

Photo by AK Photos

▲ **Tables** │ 2004

25 x 40 x 20 inches
(63.5 x 101.6 x 50.8 cm)
Maple

Photo by AK Photos

▲ **Pair of Teapots** | 2004

6 x 11 x 7 inches
(15.2 x 27.9 x 17.8 cm)
Maple

Photo by AK Photos

" The textures and surfaces created by turning wet wood will always be difficult to interpret. My reverence for wood always grounds me. "

William Moore

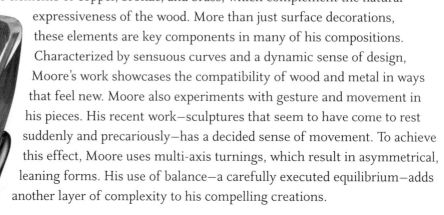

USING THE PROCESSES OF WOODTURNING AND METAL SPINNING to explore three-dimensional form, William Moore produces work that has an elegant simplicity. His vessels and sculptural objects feature elements of copper, bronze, and brass, which complement the natural expressiveness of the wood. More than just surface decorations, these elements are key components in many of his compositions. Characterized by sensuous curves and a dynamic sense of design, Moore's work showcases the compatibility of wood and metal in ways that feel new. Moore also experiments with gesture and movement in his pieces. His recent work—sculptures that seem to have come to rest suddenly and precariously—has a decided sense of movement. To achieve this effect, Moore uses multi-axis turnings, which result in asymmetrical, leaning forms. His use of balance—a carefully executed equilibrium—adds another layer of complexity to his compelling creations.

◀ **Nehalem Vessel** | 2005
13½ x 11 x 10 inches
(34.3 x 27.9 x 25.4 cm)
Madrone burl, blackwood
Photo by Dan Kvitka

Copper Section | 2005 ▶

11 x 12 x 12 inches
(27.9 x 30.5 x 30.5 cm)
Mahogany
Photo by Bill Bachhuber

◀ **Lean In** | 2005

16 x 35 x 32 inches
(40.6 x 88.9 x 81.3 cm)
Madrone burl
Photo by Dan Kvitka

▲ **Syros** | 2001

11½ x 11½ x 11½ inches
(29.2 x 29.2 x 29.2 cm)
Madrone burl
Photo by Harold Wood

" Junctions, transitions, how all the parts fit together and work together to make a complete piece—these are underlying themes in many of my creations. "

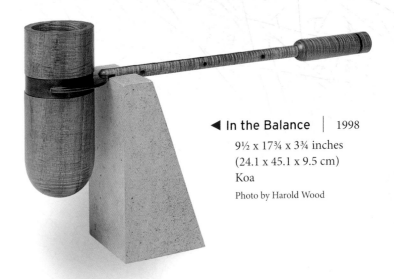

▲ **Aragon** | 1998

20 x 17 x 12 inches
(50.8 x 43.2 x 30.5 cm)
Myrtle
Photo by Harold Wood

◀ **In the Balance** | 1998

9½ x 17¾ x 3¾ inches
(24.1 x 45.1 x 9.5 cm)
Koa
Photo by Harold Wood

Willamette Pitcher | 2007 ▶

7¾ x 11 x 5¾ inches
(19.7 x 27.9 x 14.6 cm)
Oak
Photo by Dan Kvitka

" I usually start a new work by imagining what form will take best advantage of a given piece of wood. It might be the grain or it might be the form of a piece that suggests the best way to proceed. "

◀ **Cornucopia** | 1999
11½ x 23¼ x 10½ inches
(29.2 x 59.1 x 26.7 cm)
Madrone burl
Photo by Harold Wood

▲ **Seed Pod** | 2003

6½ x 6½ x 15 inches
(16.5 x 16.5 x 38.1 cm)
Oak burl

Photo by Harold Wood

▲ **Gatherer Series** | 1999

14 x 8 inches
(35.6 x 20.3 cm)
Maple burl, mahogany

Photo by Harold Wood

▲ Ochoco | 2005

9½ x 23 x 12 inches
(24.1 x 58.4 x 30.5 cm)
Buckeye burl

Photo by Dan Kvitka

" Being a teacher at an art college has had a major influence on my work. I constantly talk to my students about form, mass, and line. These concepts find expression in my own work. "

▲ **Lidded Orb** | 2006

10½ x 11 x 12 inches
(26.7 x 27.9 x 30.5 cm)
Mahogany, ebony

Photo by Dan Kvitka

David Ellsworth

REFLECTING HIS REVERENCE FOR THE VESSEL FORM, David Ellsworth's work represents an exploration of both surfaces and interiors. Ellsworth challenges viewers to experience wood as a membrane that defines the volume of energy within. Operating on the principle that form should not be overwhelmed by material or technique, he creates bowls and vessels that have a distinctive purity. Ellsworth uses his work to explore the beauty of more common species of woods, many of which he finds on his property in Pennsylvania. He takes a minimalist approach to the creative process, using no finishes and only limited surface manipulation. Cutting spalted—or rotted—wood so efficiently that he achieves a smooth surface without sanding allows him to show his pieces in their natural state without a finish. The flaws and surface characteristics of the material thus become important parts of Ellsworth's designs.

◀ **Bowl** | 1979
2½ x 8½ x 8½ inches
(6.4 x 21.6 x 21.6 cm)
Brazilian rosewood
Photo by artist

▲ **Ash Pot** | 2005

9 x 6 x 6 inches
(22.9 x 15.2 x 15.2 cm)
Black ash burl

Photo by artist

◀ **Black Pot–Tall** │ 1996

13 x 13 x 13 inches
(33 x 33 x 33 cm)
Ash

Photo by artist

Black Pot Dawn #3 │ 1999 ▶

10 x 8 inches
(25.4 x 20.3 cm)
Ash

Photo by artist

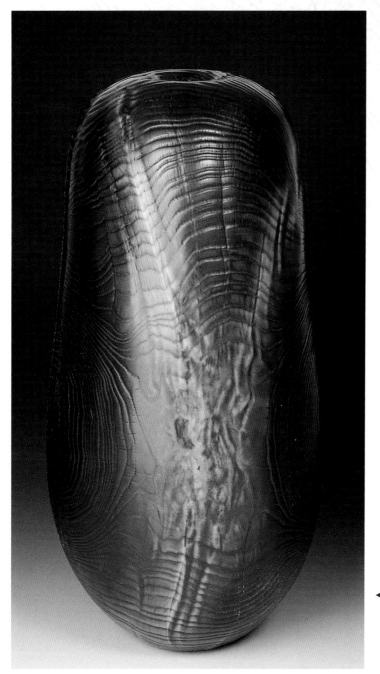

" As a maker, I find myself drawn to the interior of a form, because it's there that I discover the origin of its force and its spirit. "

◄ **Black Pot Dawn #14** | 2000
16½ x 9 x 9 inches
(41.9 x 22.9 x 22.9 cm)
Ash

Photo by artist

▲ **Stratum Sphere** │ 1999

　6¼ x 6¼ x 6¼ inches
　(15.9 x 15.9 x 15.9 cm)
　Spalted maple
　Photo by artist

▲ **Beech Pot–Tall** │ 2004

　16 x 7 x 7 inches
　(40.6 x 17.8 x 17.8 cm)
　Spalted English beech
　Photo by artist

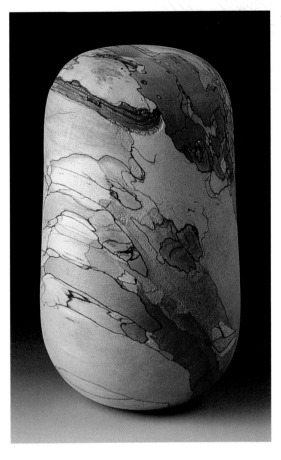

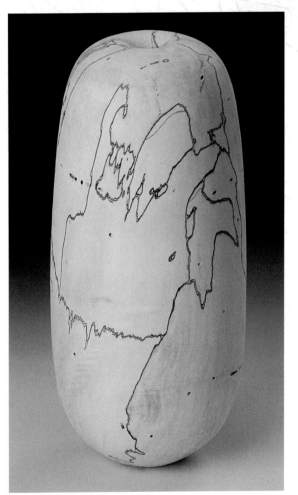

◄ Homage Pot #11 | 1999

9 x 5½ x 5½ inches
(22.9 x 14 x 14 cm)
Spalted maple

Photo by artist

" The sphere has long been a primary source of inspiration for my designs. Whether stretched, squeezed, shifted, pulled, or pushed, this universal symbol remains a constant resource for the type of energy that I try to bring to my work. "

▲ Homage Pot #31 | 2002

10 x 4½ x 4½ inches
(25.4 x 11.4 x 11.4 cm)
Spalted maple

Photo by artist

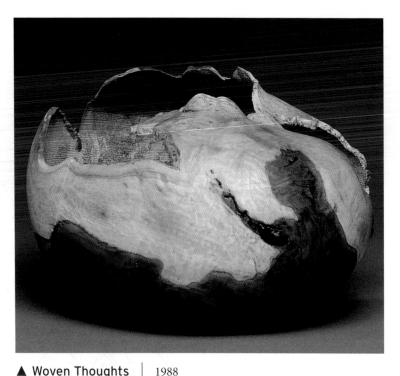

> **"** I use the surfaces of my forms not just to show off wood but to express ideas that have inspired me since childhood: the surface of an adobe home; the atmospheric transparency of night emerging into dawn; the movement of the self through time. **"**

▲ **Woven Thoughts** | 1988

16 x 22 x 22 inches
(40.6 x 55.9 x 55.9 cm)
Claro walnut burl

Photo by artist

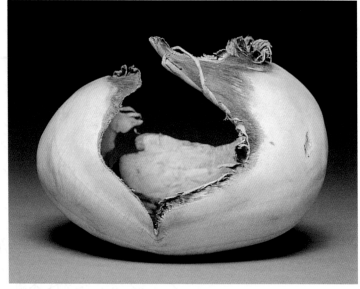

Vessel | 1982 ▶

4½ x 6 x 6 inches
(11.4 x 15.2 x 15.2 cm)
Walnut sapwood burl

Photo by artist

▲ Calypso Sphere | 2004

13 x 13 x 13 inches
(33 x 33 x 33 cm)
Black oak burl

Photo by artist

Stephen Hogbin

BOLD EXPERIMENTATION AND MASTER

CRAFTSMANSHIP come together in the work
of Stephen Hogbin. Exploring the design possibilities
contained within conventional forms—tables, bowls, and chairs—
Hogbin cuts and fragments traditional pieces, then reassembles them
into ingenious new creations. The result is work that's exceptional
both for its utility and its aesthetic appeal. Hogbin is courageous when
it comes to the reconfiguration of everyday items. His interior design
projects, including cleanly executed staircases and sleek, streamlined
cabinetry, blend technical innovation with a clear sense of context and a
modern sensibility. Hogbin has said that he is less interested in technical
matters than in design issues. His remarkable design abilities are expressed
through his selection of materials and combinations of nontraditional
forms. Unpredictable and delightful, Hogbin's work is the manifestation
of a distinctive vision and an extraordinary instinct for what's possible
with wood.

Fragmenting S. Play | 2004 ▶
35 x 20 x 13 inches
(88.9 x 50.8 x 33 cm)
Ash birch
Photo by artist

◀ **Walking Bowl** | 1999

12 x 12 x 13 inches
(30.5 x 30.5 x 33 cm)
Maple

Photo by artist

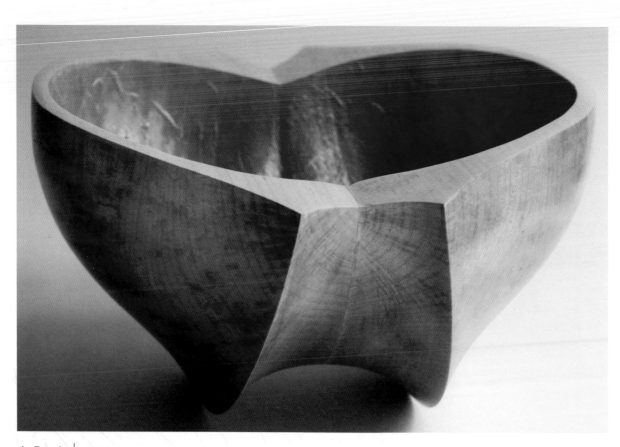

▲ Bowl | 2007
8 x 8½ inches
(20.3 x 21.6 cm)
Maple
Photo by artist

> " When it's going well, the creative process can be hair-raising, spine-tingling, mind-blowing, stimulating fun. "

▲ **Square Dance** | 2003–2004

10 x 10 x 8 inches
(25.4 x 25.4 x 20.3 cm)
Jarrah

Photo by artist

▲ **Carnival Bowl** | 2001

7 x 6½ x 8 inches
(17.8 x 16.5 x 20.3 cm)
Red elm

Photo by artist

" Work is really the wrong word for my activity. For me, the process of creation is about a search for relevance, insight, pleasure, and meaning. "

▲ **Spiral Staircase and Newel Post** | 2004

60 x 6 x 6 inches
(152.4 x 15.2 x 15.2 cm)
Ash

Photo by artist

▲ **Squash Court Railing** | 2003

36 x 144 x 8 inches
(91.4 x 365.7 x 20.3 x cm)
Ash

Photo by artist

Newel Post | 2004 ▶

74 x 6 x 6 inches
(187 x 15.2 x 15.2 cm)
Ash

Photo by artist

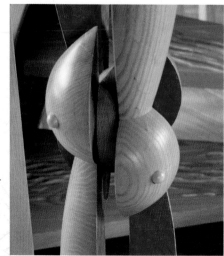

STEPHEN HOGBIN

◀ **Dac Nomad** | 2006

35 x 22½ x 20 inches
(88.9 x 57.2 x 50.8 cm)
Ash

Photo by artist

▲ **What the Bees Saw** | 2002

13 x 8 x 8 inches
(33 x 20.3 x 20.3 cm)
Rose alder

Photo by artist

" Ideas often lie quietly in the back of my mind until the circumstances are ripe.

Occasionally, an idea is so out there that it just has to be made and experienced fully. "

▲ Cedar Chair (One of Two) | 1974

34 x 28 x 40 inches
(86.4 x 71.1 x 101.6 cm)
Western red cedar
Photo by artist

▲ Set Up: The Space of a Chair | 2006

34½ x 20 x 20 inches
(87.6 x 50.8 x 50.8 cm)
Maple
Photo by artist

Ron Layport

CREATING STYLIZED FIGURES THAT SUGGEST A TIE TO ANCIENT THEMES and primal urges, Ron Layport celebrates nature with his work. His multi-figured compositions feature animals and insects, which are rendered in fine detail and possess a wonderful energy.

Layport, who views the traditional vessel as a point of departure, says that he thinks sculpturally and turns sculpturally, an attitude that shows in his bowls and decorative pieces. All design elements—color, texture, and form—come together in his work, creating a sense of harmony and quiet refinement. His pieces, constructed from multiple pieces of wood or bent to achieve curves, are often assumed to be assemblages, but in reality, each form is sculpted from a single piece of wood directly as it comes off the lathe, complete with extensions and curves. Layport's work represents a beautiful balance of texture, coloration, and form.

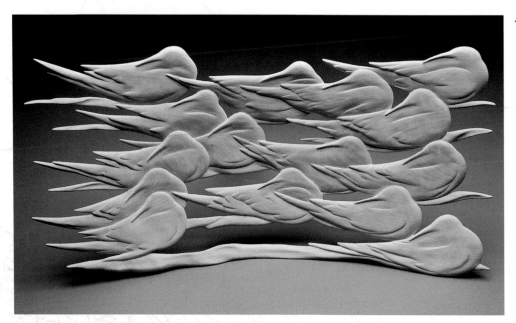

◀ Sand Shadows | 2005

13 x 27 x 3½ inches
(33 x 68.6 x 8.9 cm)
Maple

Photo by Chuck Fuhrer

▲ **Dragon Song** | 2007

10 x 8¾ inches
(25.4 x 22.2 cm)
Maple

Photo by Chuck Fuhrer

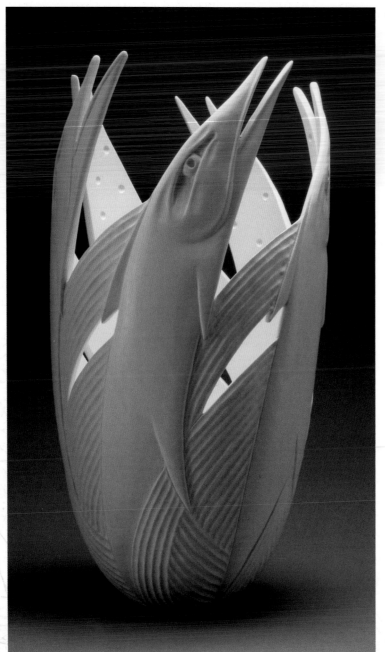

◀ **River Dancers** │ *2007*

12½ x 6¾ inches
(31.8 x 17.1 cm)
Sycamore

Photo by Chuck Fuhrer

◀ **Silk Morning** | 2005

14½ x 8½ inches
(36.8 x 21.6 cm)
Maple

Photo by Chuck Fuhrer

" Animal effigy figures have inspired utilitarian vessels since the earliest forms of human expression. I try to bring my own voice to this ongoing dialogue. "

Spirit Whites on Sky Blue Pale | 2006 ▶

10¼ x 9 inches (26 x 22.9 cm)
Maple

Photo by Chuck Fuhrer

RON LAYPORT

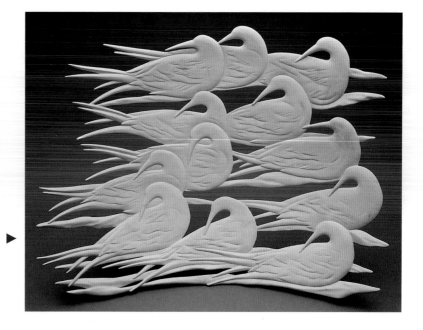

Dreamers' Bowl | 2006 ▶

19½ x 25½ x 4½ inches
(49.5 x 64.8 x 11.4 cm)
Maple

Photo by Chuck Fuhrer

Flutterbowl | 2005 ▶

16 x 24½ x 4 inches
(40.6 x 62.2 x 10.2 cm)
Cherry

Photo by Chuck Fuhrer

◀ **Windscape** | 2005

27 x 25 x 4 inches
(68.6 x 63.5 x 10.2 cm)
Cherry
Photo by Chuck Fuhrer

" I feel an affinity with the nameless makers
who came before me. I believe that the need to
make things with our hands is a core instinct,
like eating. It's part of the human condition **"**

Wolf Dance | 2007 ▶

5¼ x 19½ inches
(13.3 x 49.5 cm)
Maple
Photos by Chuck Fuhrer

◀ Walhalla │ 2004

3¾ x 16 inches
(9.5 x 40.6 cm)
Maple burl
Photo by Chuck Fuhrer

" The turned form must be purely valid as a form
before I spend time and effort on sculpting it.
I live with final turned pieces for months
sometimes before proceeding. "

▲ Incarnation of the Salmon King │ 2006

14¼ x 11 x 7 inches
(36.2 x 27.9 x 17.8 cm)
Sycamore, ebony
Photo by Chuck Fuhrer

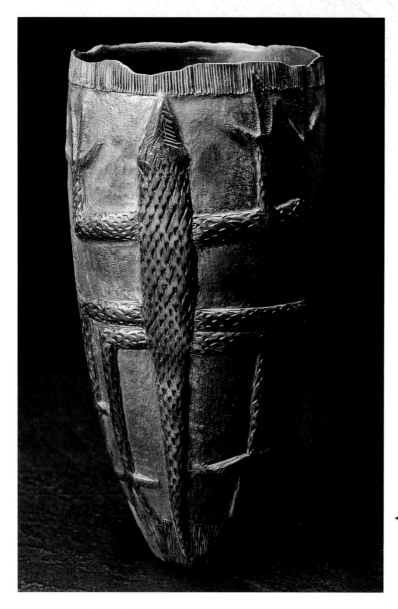

◀ **Lizards Dancing** | 2004
9½ x 4¾ inches
(24.1 x 12.1 cm)
Maple
Photo by Chuck Fuhrer

William Hunter

"SUBTRACTIVE SCULPTURING" is how William Hunter describes the process he uses to create his innovative vessels. This painstaking reduction of wood has allowed him to open up the vessel form and play with space in innovative ways. His basket-inspired vessels have surfaces that are disc-cut so that light can pass through. Their precisely carved exteriors set up provocative contrasts—between inside and outside, shadow and light, matter and empty space. Other pieces redefine the vessel shape in a dramatic fashion, transforming the traditional form into a sculptural object. Hunter's trademarks—spirals and helixes—appear repeatedly in his vessels, lending a unique energy and sense of motion to the work. Whether abstract or traditional, his vessels demonstrate the power of contrasts—and the magic of subtraction.

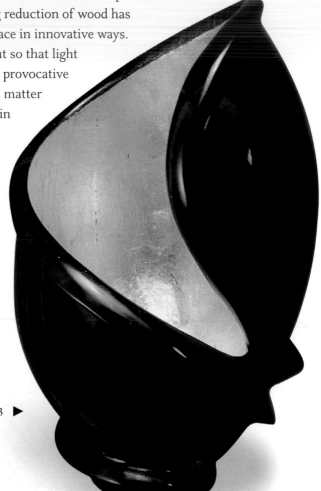

Imperial Dragon Egg #2 | 1983 ▶

6 x 4 inches
(15.2 x 10.2 cm)
Ebony
Photo by Bob Barrett

◀ **Arabian Nights** | 1989

7 x 4 inches
(17.8 x 10.2 cm)
Ebony

Photo by George Post

◀ **Kinetic Weave 33** │ 1997

7 x 10¾ inches
(17.8 x 27.3 cm)
Cocobolo

Photo by Hap Sakwa

◀ **Staccato Flutes II** │ 1991

5 x 15 inches
(12.7 x 38.1 cm)
Cocobolo

Photo by George Post

◀ **Fast Grass** | 1995

4 x 8 inches
(10.2 x 20.3 cm)
Cocobolo
Photo by George Post

" I thrive on the challenge of workmanship, of risk. I love the adrenaline and focus required. I sculpt to convey abstract energy. **"**

Phantom Vessel III | 1989 ▶

9 x 10 inches
(22.9 x 25.4 cm)
Cocobolo
Photo by George Post

WILLIAM HUNTER

"This type of work is total improvisation, an intimate dance with the material that cannot be preconceived or drawn."

▲ **Quiet Chaos** │ 2006
18 x 9 inches
(45.7 x 22.9 cm)
Cocobolo
Photo by Tony Cunha

▲ **Creation** │ 2005
26 x 26⅛ x 18 inches
(66 x 66.3 x 45.7 cm)
Australian jarrah burl
Photo by Hap Sakwa

▲ **Free Vessel** | 2003

12 x 14 x 19 inches
(30.5 x 35.6 x 48.3 cm)
Cocobolo
Photo by Alan Shaffer

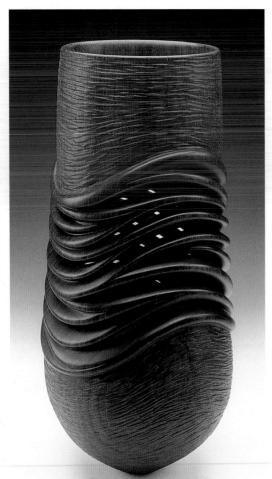

▲ **Glimmer Through Crosscurrents** | 2006

15 x 7 inches
(38.1 x 17.8 cm)
Cocobolo
Photo by Tony Cunha

▲ **Sea Garden** | 2003

16¼ x 7¾ inches
(41.3 x 19.7 cm)
Cocobolo
Photo by Alan Shaffer

▲ **Macassar Blossom** | 2007

7 x 15 inches
(17.8 x 38.1 cm)
Macassar ebony

Photo by Tony Cunha

" I use form, line, color, light, and shadow as silent voices in my work to create intrigue, to express ideas, and to relay excitement. I want the viewer to feel an emotional resonance with my world. **"**

Ron Fleming

USING CLASSICAL WOODCARVING TECHNIQUES, Ron Fleming produces freeform organic shapes characterized by smooth polished surfaces and crisp flowing edges. Formal and refined, his pieces are inspired by nature and feature floral and plant motifs. The carving process comes naturally to Fleming, who says that he lets the wood guide him as he works. Led by instinct, he creates pieces that are remarkable for their vitality, fluidity, and suppleness, and for their softly textured, sensuous lines. What Fleming calls the "aliveness" of the wood is part of what he likes about his art, and it shines through in each of his pieces. Fleming has worked as a professional illustrator, and his skill in this area is reflected in the accuracy and realism of his creations. His work has an energy all its own—a special vibrancy that compels the viewer to stop and take a closer look.

◀ **The Guardian** | 2003

38½ x 14 inches
(97.8 x 35.6 cm)
Walnut

Photo by artist

▲ **Dragon Dance** | 2001

17 x 19 inches
(43.2 x 48.3 cm)
Redwood burl

Photo by Bob Hawks

Fern Platter | 2006 ▶

5 x 24 inches
(12.7 x 61 cm)
Redwood burl

Photo by artist

◀ **Medusa** | 1998

20 x 9½ inches
(50.8 x 24.1 cm)
Cocobolo

Photo by artist

▲ **African Fern Basket** | 2007

21 x 19½ inches
(53.3 x 49.5 cm)
Redwood burl

Photo by artist

" Attending an art opening and seeing how other artists are able to extract emotion from viewers is very inspiring to me. **"**

◀ **Fandango** | 2005

17 x 7½ inches
(43.2 x 19.1 cm)
Redwood burl
Photo by artist

FLEMING

Athena | 2006 ▶

10 x 7 inches
(25.4 x 17.8 cm)
Pink ivory

Photo by artist

▲ **Leopard Flower** | 2007

12 x 15 inches
(30.5 x 38.1 cm)
Sycamore
Photo by artist

Fishhook | 2002 ▶

12 x 7½ inches
(30.5 x 19.1 cm)
Hackberry
Photo by artist

RON FLEMING

▲ **Tradescantia** | 2003
16 x 7 x 4 inches
(40.6 x 17.8 x 10.2 cm)
Basswood
Photo by artist

" I was taught not to copy the work of other artists, so I decided that I would use nature as the backbone for my work—not to copy it necessarily, but to re-style it as I envision it to be. "

▲ **Yama Yuri** | 2000
36 x 17 inches
(91.4 x 43.2 cm)
Basswood
Photo by Bob Hawks

▲ **Debona** | 1999

14 x 12 inches
(35.6 x 30.5 cm)
Bleached mahogany

Photo by Bob Hawks

Bud Latven

NEGATIVE SPACE IS A CENTRAL DESIGN CONCEPT in Bud Latven's deconstructed turned forms. Characterized by sweeping lines, irregular patterns, and fragmented sections, his sculptural objects are complex, dynamic, and innovative. Opening out the bottom of his forms—many of which are based on rotated curves and conic sections—allows Latven to explore the concepts of disintegration and fragmentation. Randomly placed contrasting elements and sections activate his pieces. In addition to large sculptural objects, Latven produces small-scale bowls and vessels. Unlike his carved, fragmented sculptures, which he makes from small segments of wood, he produces the vessels from single pieces of wood. Experiments with texture and scale have also led him to work in bronze. Full of movement, color, and energy, Latven's work represents a seamless relationship between content and form.

◀ **Tigerstone Fragment** | 1998
9 x 16 x 12 inches
(22.9 x 40.6 x 30.5 cm)
Tiger maple
Photo by artist

▲ **Maple Torsion** | 1999

16 x 17 x 11½ inches
(40.6 x 43.2 x 29.2 cm)
Tiger maple, cocobolo

Photo by artist

◀ **Bubinga Fragment** | 1997

9 x 12 x 16 inches
(22.9 x 30.5 x 40.6 cm)
African bubinga

Photo by artist

Cocobolo Torsion | 2001 ▶

19½ x 19½ x 14 inches
(49.5 x 49.5 x 35.6 cm)
Cocobolo

Photo by artist

◀ **Tulipwood Torsion** │ 2001

19½ x 19½ x 12 inches
(49.5 x 49.5 x 30.5 cm)
Brazilian tulipwood

Photo by artist

" Finishing a piece of artwork is like
coming to a junction in the road—it's not
a destination but a position from which to
evaluate new potential. "

◀ **Cristobal Torsion** │ 2000

16 x 16 x 13 inches
(40.6 x 40.6 x 33 cm)
Cristobal

Photo by artist

BUD LATVEN

Spiral Impact 2 | 2007 ▶

20 x 24 x 24 inches
(50.8 x 61 x 61 cm)
Cocobolo, tiger maple
Photos by artist

Dancing Impact 3 | 2007 ▶

21 x 26 x 26 inches
(53.3 x 66 x 66 cm)
Cocobolo, tiger maple
Photo by artist

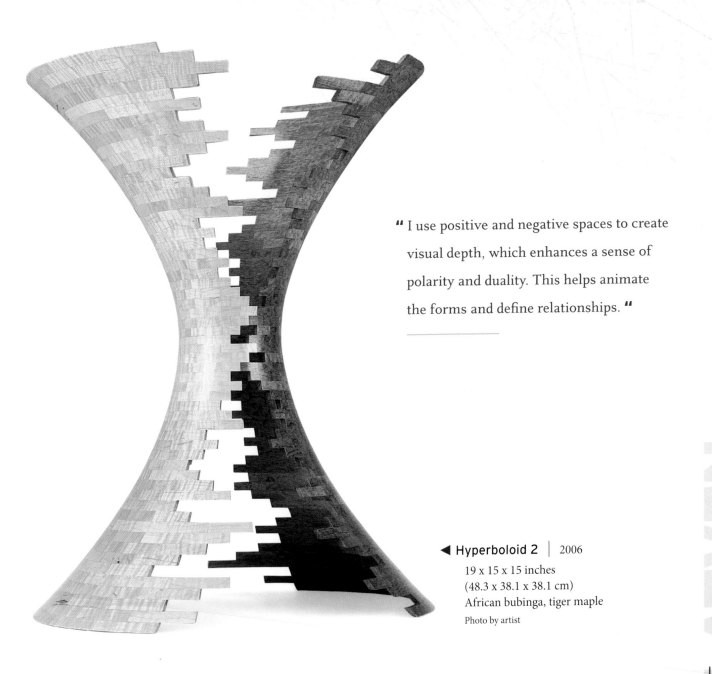

" I use positive and negative spaces to create visual depth, which enhances a sense of polarity and duality. This helps animate the forms and define relationships. "

◀ **Hyperboloid 2** | 2006

19 x 15 x 15 inches
(48.3 x 38.1 x 38.1 cm)
African bubinga, tiger maple

Photo by artist

▲ **Brazilian Sunrise** | 2006

16 x 17 x 17 inches
(40.6 x 43.2 x 43.2 cm)
Brazilian satinwood,
Brazilian purpleheart
Photo by artist

" My current work focuses on
carved geometric forms from the
mathematics of nature. "

▲ **Red Tower** | 1994

16 x 7½ x 7½ inches
(40.6 x 19.1 x 19.1 cm)
Brazilian tulipwood, African ebony
Photo by artist

▲ Fractured Tower │ 2002

16 x 10½ x 16 inches
(40.6 x 26.7 x 40.6 cm)
Tiger maple, rosewood,
tulipwood

Photos by artist

VESERY

Jacques Vesery

STIRRED BY THE DIVINE PROPORTIONS OF NATURAL FORMS, Jacques Vesery creates organic, highly textured vessels and decorative objects that are models of technical virtuosity. The finely detailed surfaces of his pieces command the viewer's attention. Working with color—establishing contrasting or complementary relationships—is a critical part of his creative process. After carving a piece with a burning tool, he coats it with India ink to create a uniformly colored surface. Then he applies layers of acrylic paint, adding five or ten coats in different colors in order to increase the depth of his carvings. Leaves, seashells, and waves inspire Vesery and serve as his touchstones, as they reflect nature's perfection. A willingness to go deep—to search for and recreate the perfect detail—is part of what makes his work so unforgettable.

◀ **On a Dark Wing of a Wave** | 2007
4 x 2½ inches
(10.2 x 6.4 cm)
Cherry
Photo by artist

▲ **Sleeping with Angels** | 2007

4 x 6½ inches
(10.2 x 16.5 cm)
Mahogany, cherry

Photo by artist

A Celadon Sky Dream | 2006 ▶

2½ x 5 inches
(6.4 x 12.7 cm)
Cherry
Photo by artist

◀ **Makana Ka Na Hoku** | 2006–2007

2½ x 5 inches
(6.4 x 12.7 cm)
Cherry
Photos by artist

Of Sea and Sky | 2004 ▶

5½ x 2½ inches
(14 x 6.4 cm)
Cherry

Photo by Robert Diamante

◀ **The Enigma from Within** | 2006

2½ x 2³⁄₁₆ inches
(6.4 x 5.6 cm)
Cherry

Photos by artist

▲ **Raising an American Dream** | 2006

2 x 16 inches
(5.1 x 40.6 cm)
Swiss pear, holly, ash
Photo by artist

" Craft is based on functionality;

art is based on spirituality. "

Endless Currents | 2004 ▶

6 x 4½ inches
(15.2 x 11.4 cm)
Cherry, jabin burl
Photo by artist

▲ **On a Celadon Wing** | 2005

2³/₁₆ x 5 inches
(5.6 x 12.7 cm)
Cherry, ebony
Photo by artist

" I am always trying to convey something in my work, but I'm rarely willing to voice the message. I would much rather hear what my work means to others. "

> "Exploring texture exposes our minds to the wonders of hidden beauty around us in every part of life."

▲ **Bark at the Moon** | 2005

5½ x 4³/₁₆ x 6½ inches
(14 x 10.7 x 16.5 cm)
Cherry, boxwood burl, maple

Photo by artist

Phlight of Phancy | 2001 ▶

4 x 4 inches
(10.2 x 10.2 cm)
Cherry, ebony

Photo by Robert Diamante

A Little Time to Fly | 2005 ▶

3½ x 3 x 2 inches
(8.9 x 7.6 x 5.1 cm)
Cherry, blackwood burl

Photo by artist

Betty Scarpino

REMINISCENT OF ANCIENT FERTILITY OBJECTS, Betty Scarpino's abstract figures are often marked by sensuous curves and a unique voluptuousness. Scarpino started out making functional pieces but wanted to take on new challenges as her career progressed. Her move into non-functional abstract forms seems only natural, given the clean organic shapes and uniquely feminine forms she produces. She incorporates line into her sculptures by adding grooves and beads, and while Scarpino is in the carving phase, these lines serve as a focus for movement and contrast. In the finished sculptures, however, the grooves and beads are often reduced to a minimum. The finished products have a sense of lyricism, with carved flowing lines that give them a quality of motion.

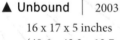

▲ **Unbound** | 2003
16 x 17 x 5 inches
(40.6 x 43.2 x 12.7 cm)
Walnut

Photo by Judy Ditmer

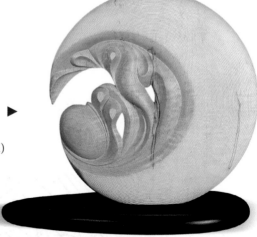

Watershed | 2003 ▶
16 x 18 x 5 inches
(40.6 x 45.7 x 12.7 cm)
Maple

Photo by Judy Ditmer

▲ **Response to Old Devotions** | 2003

19 x 17 x 9 inches
(48.3 x 43.2 x 22.9 cm)
Sycamore

Photo by Judy Ditmer

Familiar Strangers | 2000 ▶

12 x 16 x 2½ inches
(30.5 x 40.6 x 6.4 cm)
Maple, poplar

Photo by Judy Ditmer

" I'm drawn to the use of wood
because it's a warm, responsive
material that allows for an infinite
expression of ideas. "

◀ **Crossroads** | 2001

16 x 14 x 7 inches
(40.6 x 35.6 x 17.8 cm)
Maple

Photo by Judy Ditmer

▲ **Gather the Wind** | 2007

16 x 16 x 4 inches
(40.6 x 40.6 x 10.2 cm)
Maple

Photo by Shawn Spence

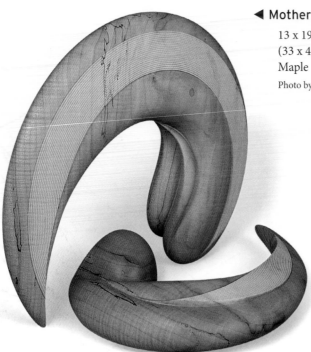

◀ **Mother Bridge** | 2000

13 x 19 x 5 inches
(33 x 48.3 x 12.7 cm)
Maple
Photo by Judy Ditmer

" Yes, the lathe produces round objects.

To that, I say, 'Embrace the limitations!'

Discovery is critical to how I work. **"**

▲ **Inviolate Portal** | 2007

14 x 13 x 5 inches
(35.6 x 33 x 12.7 cm)
Ash
Photo by Shawn Spence

BETTY **SCARPINO**

▲ Glory! June! | 1996
7 x 9 x 9 inches
(17.8 x 22.9 x 22.9 cm)
Maple
Photo by Judy Ditmer

" It's fascinating to find new ways of deconstructing, then reconstructing a turned form. It requires that I consider objects in new ways, be playful, and think outside the circle. "

Reverberations | 2000 ▶

15 x 14 x 3½ inches
(38.1 x 35.6 x 8.9 cm)
Walnut

Photo by Judy Ditmer

◀ **Containing Desire** | 2004

17 x 15 x 3 inches
(43.2 x 38.1 x 7.6 cm)
Maple, poplar

Photo by Judy Ditmer

▲ **Still Desire** | 2004

13 x 18 x 10 inches
(33 x 45.7 x 25.4 cm)
Ash

Photo by Judy Ditmer

Jean-François Escoulen

A MASTER OF MULTI-AXIS TURNING, Jean-François Escoulen creates whimsical, one-of-a-kind, humorous works that reflect his own unique vision. Multi-axis turning was an uncommon procedure before Escoulen began using it. To facilitate the technique, he invented a special chuck that allowed him to push the limits of the lathe and create unusual shapes with the gouge. Characterized by crisp flowing lines, complex interconnected surfaces, and a pronounced delicacy, his pieces have expanded the possibilities of the multi-axis technique. Balanced and beautiful, his work is suggestive without being literally representational, bringing to mind machines, birds, and toys. These delightfully off-kilter creations feature different shapes made from various types of woods. Escoulen, who says he is obsessed with defying the laws of gravity, has his own aesthetic—a mix of the futuristic and the classic that defies categorization.

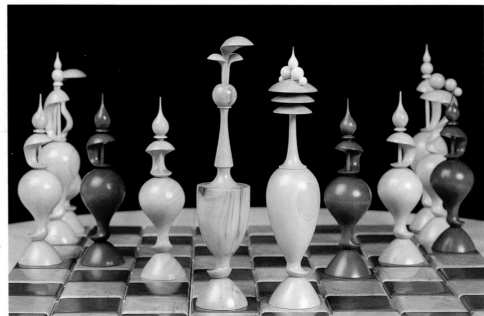

Chess Set | 2005 ▶
29½ x 31½ inches
(75 x 80 cm)
Boxwood, maple
Photos by Yves Duble

◀ **Any Eggs?** │ 2005

Height, 13¾ inches (35 cm)
Boxwood, ebony,
elm burl

Photo by Yves Duble

Don't Touch My Egg │ 2004 ▶

Height, 19^{11}/$_{16}$ inches (50 cm)
Elm heather, cherry

Photo by Yves Duble

◀ **Chicken Family** | 2004

Height, 22 1/16 inches (56 cm)
Cypress, boxwood, elm burl
Photo by John Hill

◀ **Untitled** | 2005

Height, 21 5/8 inches (55 cm)
Maple, boxwood, pink ivory
Photo by Yves Duble

" My goal has always been to discover
the possibilities of shape and technique
on the lathe. I enjoy looking for balance
in seemingly unbalanced shapes. "

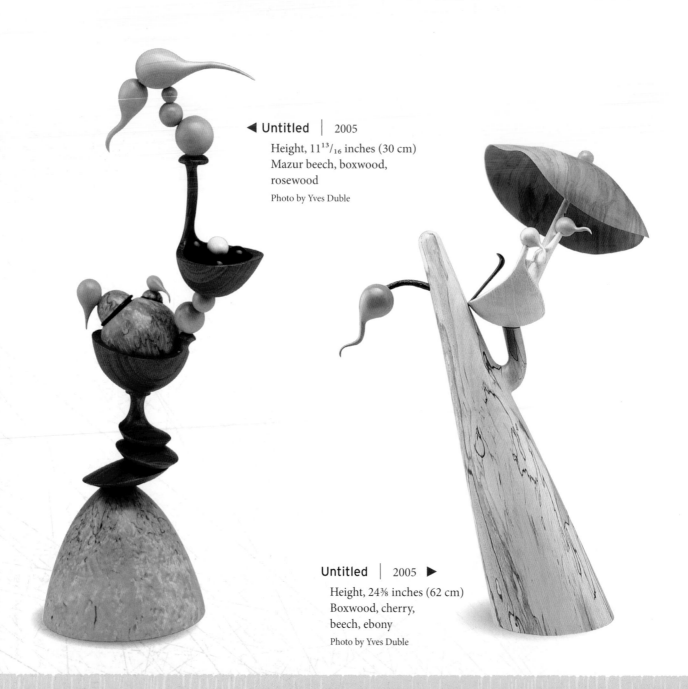

ESCOULEN

◀ **Untitled** │ 2005

Height, 11¹³/₁₆ inches (30 cm)
Mazur beech, boxwood,
rosewood

Photo by Yves Duble

Untitled │ 2005 ▶

Height, 24⅜ inches (62 cm)
Boxwood, cherry,
beech, ebony

Photo by Yves Duble

" My work has moved towards eccentric turning, but sometimes the most unusual pieces reveal my traditional training. "

◀ **Contemplation** | 2005

Height, 23⅝ inches (60 cm)
Ash, boxwood, maple
Photo by Yves Duble

▲ **Box** | 2004

Height, 11 inches (28 cm)
Osage orange, boxwood
Photo by artist

◀ **Triplets** | 2005

Height, 9¹³/₁₆ inches (25 cm)
Cherry, pink ivory
Photo by Yves Duble

◀ **The Guard** | 2004
Height, 11¹³/₁₆ inches (30 cm)
Osage orange
Photo by Yves Duble

▲ **Balance Game** | 2003
Height, 13¾ inches (35 cm)
Rosewood, boxwood
Photo by Yves Duble

" After admiring the ornamental works of the seventeenth and

eighteenth centuries and reproducing pieces from the past,

I wanted to move on to something else: creativity combined

with new techniques. **"**

Steve Sinner

ADDING A MODERN TWIST TO THE TRADITIONAL DECORATED VESSEL, Steve Sinner has broken new ground with his beautifully patterned vases and goblets. He uses wood as a canvas for geometric and graphic patterns that have a contemporary feel, yet many of his large-scale, thin-walled vessels are reminiscent of classical Greek sculpture. Using metal foil, chemical processes, gold leaf, paint, and ink, he applies intricate designs to the exteriors of his pieces with remarkable precision. With the help of a laser attachment he designed himself, he is able to control the wall thickness of his deep, hollow vessels. Sinner has developed a number of patterns that rely on rhythm and color to enhance the natural beauty of his turned forms. Cleanly constructed and beautifully embellished, Sinner's work blends technical expertise with high artistry.

Celtic Dream III │ 2001 ▶
12¼ x 7 x 7 inches
(31.1 x 17.8 x 17.8 cm)
Maple
Photo by artist

◀ **Loreto B.C.S. II** | 2006

27 x 14½ x 14½ inches
(68.6 x 36.8 x 36.8 cm)
Maple

Photos by Imaging Solutions

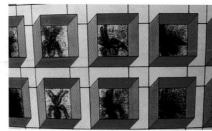

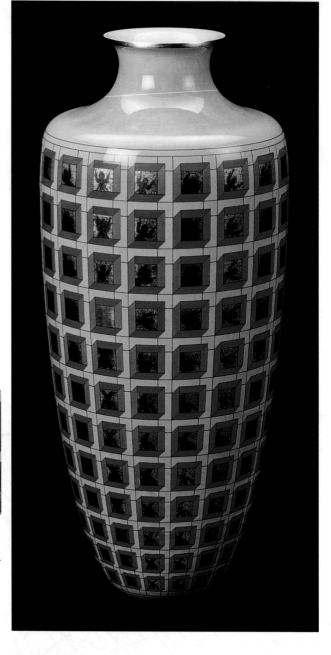

Ant Farm III | 2003 ▶

26½ x 11⅝ x 11⅝ inches
(67.3 x 29.5 x 29.5 cm)
Maple

Photos by Imaging Solutions

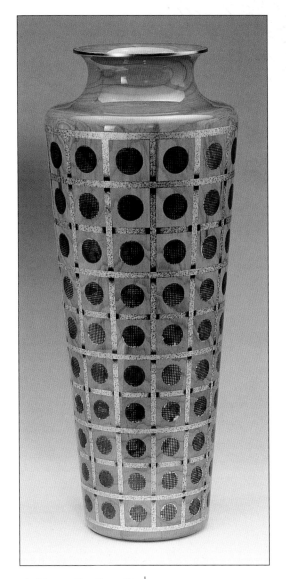

▲ Mosquito Trap II │ 2002

17¾ x 7⅛ x 7⅛ inches
(45.1 x 18.1 x 18.1 cm)
Cherry
Photo by Imaging Solutions

◀ Tall Boxes │ 2004

◀ Tall Boxes │ 2004

12⅝ x 6½ x 6½ inches
(32.1 x 16.5 x 16.5 cm)
Cherry
Photo by Imaging Solutions

" My lack of a formal art education has been
a huge plus. No one has ever shown me
what I can't or shouldn't do. "

STEVE SINNER

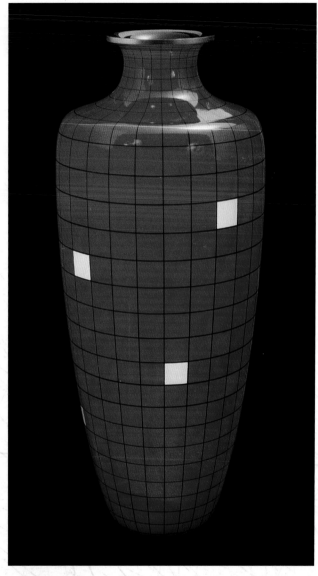

▲ **Bound in Black** | 2006

26 x 10¾ x 10¾ inches
(66 x 27.3 x 27.3 cm)
Maple

Photo by Imaging Solutions

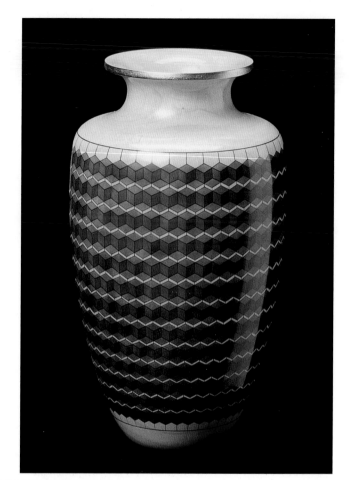

▲ **Blue Cubes** | 2005

9⅛ x 5⅛ x 5⅛ inches
(23.2 x 13 x 13 cm)
Maple

Photo by Imaging Solutions

" I usually have to force myself to work. The fear
of failure is often paralyzing. Only when a piece
begins to sing to me does the work flow easily. "

▲ **1200 Walnut Boxes** | 2004

28¾ x 13½ x 13½ inches
(73 x 34.3 x 34.3 cm)
Walnut

Photo by Imaging Solutions

▲ **The Chairman Dances** | 2006

13 x 7⅝ x 7⅝ inches
(33 x 19.4 x 19.4 cm)
Maple

Photo by Imaging Solutions

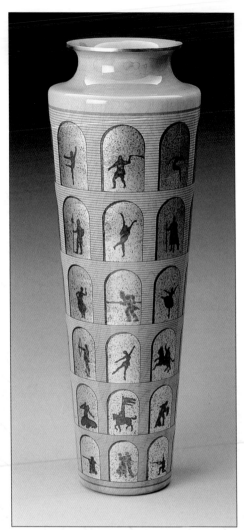

▲ **Dancers & Warriors III** | 2003

27 x 9¼ x 9¼ inches
(68.6 x 23.5 x 23.5 cm)
Maple

Photo by Imaging Solutions

▲ **Time to Say Goodbye** | 2000

15¼ x 7½ x 7½ inches
(38.7 x 19.1 x 19.1 cm)
Maple

Photo by Bob Barrett

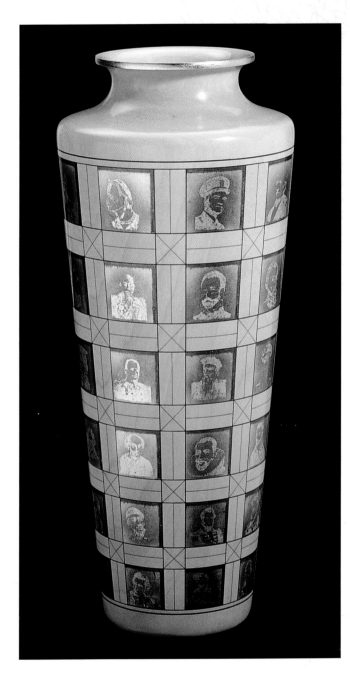

" I wince each time I hear someone say 'he has gone beyond the vessel' as a form of praise. The vessel is classic and needs to be explored as much today as it did two thousand years ago. "

◀ Seafarers │ 2004

15⅝ x 6½ x 6½ inches
(39.7 x 16.5 x 16.5 cm)
Maple

Photo by Imaging Solutions

STEVE SINNER

Giles Gilson

INFLUENCED BY EVERYTHING FROM HOT-ROD CARS to industrial engineering to music theory, Giles Gilson approaches his art with a sense of adventure. Presenting viewers with the unexpected, his work has many moods—humorous, elegant, dynamic—and is always impeccably finished. Gilson enhanced his early pieces with graphic patterns and bold colors, using pearl pigments and lacquers to achieve a smooth finish. Other pieces are heavily pierced and carved, allowing the viewer to see the interior and exterior at the same time. Embellishments of brass, stainless steel, and aluminum play important roles in ingenious works that bring to mind mechanical devices. Gilson, who says he views wood as a sculpting medium because of its warmth and dynamic color, is clearly unafraid to venture into new territory with his work.

Venus and Vargas | 2006 ▶
30 x 18 inches
(76.2 x 45.7 cm)
Basswood, pakkawood
Photo by artist

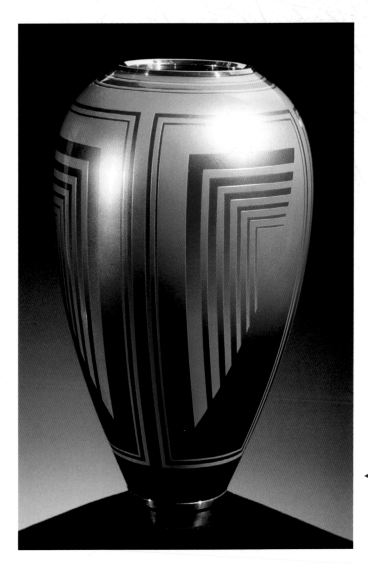

◀ Fade Reversal | 1986

13 x 7 inches
(33 x 17.8 cm)
Basswood

Photo by Rick Siciliano

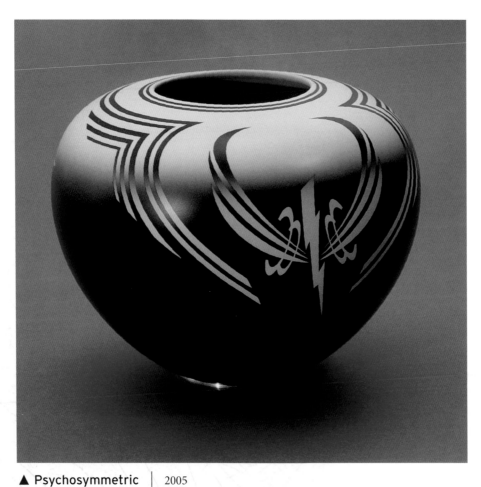

▲ **Psychosymmetric** | 2005

6 x 7½ inches
(15.2 x 19.1 cm)
Basswood

Photo by artist

" I don't really know what I'm going to do with a piece until I actually do it. What results is often a surprise. "

▲ Flower of the Open Heart | 1997

15 x 7 inches
(38.1 x 17.8 cm)
Mahogany, walnut

Photo by Kevin Wallace

◄ Cammy-Oh 2 | 2001

18 x 5 inches
(45.7 x 12.7 cm)
Basswood, walnut

Photo by artist

◄ Fleur de Compassion | 1998

21 x 7 inches
(53.3 x 17.8 cm)
Mahogany, lacquered basswood,
corian

Photo by Rick Siciliano

▲ **Energyball** | 1997

    6 x 6 x 7 inches
    (15.2 x 15.2 x 17.8 cm)
    Walnut, birch, padauk,
    composite wood
    Photo by artist

▲ **Lighting the Way** | 2001

    30 x 10 inches
    (76.2 x 25.4 cm)
    Basswood, mahogany, birch
    Photo by artist

" A useful tool for extending one's creative abilities is to practice seeing the world from a different perspective. Another useful tool is a willingness to go beyond conventional thinking. "

▲ **First Wobbledancer** | 1997

6 x 6 x 4½ inches
(15.2 x 15.2 x 11.4 cm)
Bird's-eye maple, padauk ebony,
holly, purpleheart

Photo by artist

▲ **Interpretation III** │ 1981

8 inches (20.3 cm)
Various domestic and exotic woods
Photo by Rick Siciliano

" I like to have fun with my work. I appreciate the absurd. So many aspects of existence seem ridiculous that it often feels more accurate to express absurdity than it does 'normality.' "

◄ **The Maker** | 1995
16½ x 6¼ inches
(41.9 x 15.9 cm)
Various domestic and exotic woods
Photo by Rick Siciliano

Bert Marsh

A PASSION FOR WOOD AND A

DESIRE FOR PERFECTION are two of
the forces that drive Bert Marsh. He exposes the
textures, colors, and patterns in wood, then enhances
his material with meticulous finishing. Thanks to his
highly developed sensitivity to wood, Marsh knows how
a variation in form of less than a millimeter can affect the
success of a piece. Featuring beautifully flared edges and
bold textures, his vases and bowls are clean, elegant, and
free of embellishment. Marsh has said that he finds creative
ideas for his work in everyday objects, but that he is most
inspired by wood itself. Paying particular attention to natural
defects, discoloration, and grain malformations, Marsh uses
these elements to heighten the expressive beauty of his pieces.
With walls so thin they resemble porcelain, many of his pieces
possess a unique weightlessness.

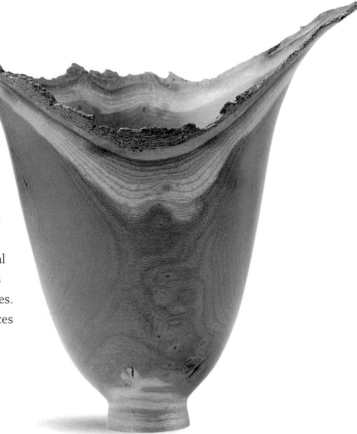

Mulberry Vase with Bark Edge | 1989 ▲
7½ x 8 x 8 inches
(19.1 x 20.3 x 20.3 cm)
Mulberry
Photo by Tony Boase

▲ **Laburnum Natural-Edged Vase** | 1995

6 x 6 x 6 inches
(15.2 x 15.2 x 15.2 cm)
Laburnum

Photo by Tony Boase

◄ **Burr Briarwood Vase** | 1995

8 x 8½ x 8½ inches
(20.3 x 21.6 x 21.6 cm)
Briarwood
Photo by Tony Boase

" Woodturning requires a range of basic skills, but those skills are merely a starting point. They must be perfected and used as a basis for experimentation if an artist's work is to express his or her own personality. "

Natural Edge Burr Briar Root Vase | 2006 ►

4¾ x 9^{1}/$_{16}$ x 9^{1}/$_{16}$ inches
(12.1 x 23 x 23 cm)
Burr briarwood
Photo by artist

▲ **Australian Grassroot Vase** | 1992

4½ x 8 x 8 inches
(11.4 x 20.3 x 20.3 cm)
Australian grassroot
Photo by Tony Boase

◀ **Burr Jarrah Vase** | 1989

7 x 6½ x 6½ inches
(17.8 x 16.5 x 16.5 cm)
Burr jarrah
Photo by Tony Boase

" Understanding wood is an
important part of being able to
work it successfully, and the
more I've learned about it, the
more I've come to appreciate
and admire it. "

Spalted Beech Bowl | 1994 ▶

3¾ x 13 x 13 inches
(9.5 x 33 x 33 cm)
Spalted beech
Photo by Tony Boase

▲ **Spalted Elm Vase** | 1990

7 x 14½ x 14½ inches
(17.8 x 36.8 x 36.8 cm)
Spalted elm

Photo by Tony Boase

African Padauk Vase | 1994 ▶

4½ x 8 x 8 inches
(11.4 x 20.3 x 20.3 cm)
Padauk

Photo by Tony Boase

▲ **Natural Edge African Blackwood Vase** | 1992

6½ x 4½ x 4½ inches
(16.5 x 11.4 x 11.4 cm)
African blackwood

Photo by Tony Boase

◄ **Natural Edge Masur Birch Vase** | 2004

5⅞ x 9⁷/₁₆ x 9⁷/₁₆ inches
(15 x 24 x 24 cm)
Masur birch
Photo by artist

" There is no complex philosophy
attached to the work I do. I'm simply
trying to achieve the perfect form—
the purest possible curves expressed in
simple, uncluttered shapes that will expose
the beauty of the wood to its fullest. "

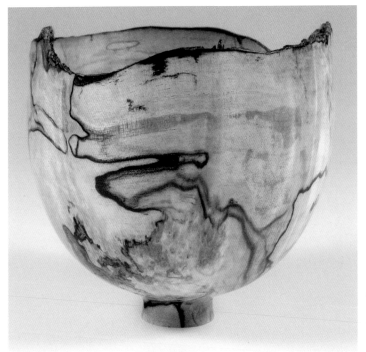

◄ **Natural Edge Spalted Horse Chestnut Vase** | 2001

5⅛ x 5⅛ x 5⅛ inches (13 x 13 x 13 cm)
Spalted horse chestnut
Photo by artist

BERT MARSH

271

Brenda Behrens

STRENGTH AND FRAGILITY: Both of these qualities are united in the intricately carved pieces of Brenda Behrens. Creating finely wrought vessels that reflect her love of embellishment, Behrens adds delicate details to her turned forms, and the result is work with an unexpected airiness. Some of her pieces feature beautifully carved blossoms, vines, and leaves—designs that are complex yet only minimally representational, that assert themselves without overwhelming the grain of the wood. The piercing and carving of just one takes Behrens 40 to 50 hours. Other pieces feature special flourishes like turned beads, feathers, and leather. Regardless of the ornamentation, Behrens' focus is always on the natural beauty of the wood. She never fails to highlight the integrity of her material, treating it as the central point of her design. With an incredible range and an enduring taste for exploration, Behrens makes work that pushes boundaries.

◀ Tender Tendrils IV | 1998
4 x 9 inches
(10.2 x 22.9 cm)
Myrtle
Photo by artist

▲ **Empress** │ 1993

6 x 9 inches
(15.2 x 22.9 cm)
Black walnut

Photo by artist

▲ **Ribbon** │ 1993

5¼ x 6½ inches
(13.3 x 16.5 cm)
Olive

Photo by artist

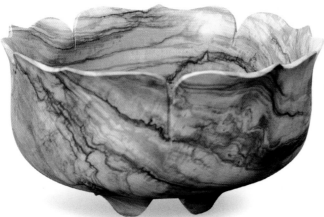

" I like to focus on the foot of a vessel and embellish it, to create a surprise for the viewer who picks up the piece and examines it. "

◀ **Piece Number 15331 Lotus** │ 1993

2½ x 3½ inches
(6.4 x 8.9 cm)
Olive
Photo by artist

Daffodil │ 1993 ▶

2½ x 6 inches
(6.4 x 15.2 cm)
Myrtle
Photo by artist

▲ **YES with Loop II** | 2002

4 x 6¼ inches
(10.2 x 15.9 cm)
Myrtle
Photo by David Peters

" My pieces are meant to be held in the hands,

so that the softness of the wood can be

appreciated and the creation itself

can be experienced. "

◀ **Twining Leaves** | 2004

6 x 5 inches
(15.2 x 12.7 cm)
Myrtle burl

Photo by David Peters

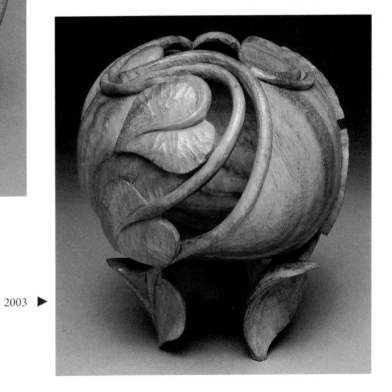

Ballet of the Leaves | 2003 ▶

4¾ x 4¼ inches
(12.1 x 10.8 cm)
Carob

Photo by David Peters

◀ **Piece Number 15103** │ 1991

4¾ x 3½ inches
(12.1 x 8.9 cm)
Black walnut

Photo by artist

Piece Number 80201 │ 1992 ▶

8½ x 5¼ inches
(21.6 x 13.3 cm)
Macassar ebony

Photo by artist

Vessel with Collar │ 1994 ▶

6¼ x 4½ inches
(15.9 x 11.4 cm)
Myrtle

Photo by artist

▲ **Dancing Leaves III** | 1992

5⅛ x 7 inches
(13 x 17.8 cm)
Myrtle
Photo by George Post

" My interest in woodturning began when I acquired an old
Sears bench-top lathe. And when I realized that I could
carve on a turned object, I felt that I had found my calling. "

David Sengel

ALTHOUGH HIS USE OF FOUND OBJECTS INITIALLY CAUSED CONTROVERSY in the woodturning community, David Sengel is now recognized as a master craftsman and innovator—an artist who paved the way for others interested in adding external materials to basic turned forms. From the rugged and natural to the elegant and refined, Sengel's bowls, urns, and sculptural presentations feature a mix of styles and moods. Locust thorns—a Sengel trademark—add an edge to his beautifully austere vessels. His bird and insect forms dazzle the viewer thanks to their one-of-a-kind design and precise detailing. Ingeniously composed, his hollow birds often feature an element of surprise—small lids in their backs or removable heads. Sengel has used black as a primary color in his work for the past two decades and has painted with a variety of substances over the years, including stove paint, shoe polish, and lacquer. Woodturning, as he practices it, is a brave exploration of form and substance.

Fish Bowl | 1995 ▶
18 x 7 inches
(45.7 x 17.8 cm)
Maple, thorns
Photo by Michael Siede

◀ **The Owl and the Frog** │ 1997

20 x 12 x 7 inches
(50.8 x 30.5 x 17.8 cm)
Cherry, maple, laurel,
rose thorns, locust thorns

Photo by Michael Siede

◀ The Ritual Shedding of Thorns │ 1999

8 x 5 inches (20.3 x 12.7 cm)
Redwood burl, dogwood,
rose thorns

Photo by Michael Siede

Family Portrait │ 2002 ▶

16 x 14 x 6 inches
(40.6 x 35.6 x 15.2 cm)
Dogwood, rose thorns,
locust thorns

Photo by Troy Tuttle

◀ **Fish Monger** | 2003

18 x 8 inches
(45.7 x 20.3 cm)
Fir, cherry, rose thorns,
locust thorns

Photo by Troy Tuttle

DAVID **SENGEL**

" Everyday objects like teacups or goblets have been a good source of ideas for me over the years. Altering or poking fun at objects that are in common use is a temptation I can't resist. "

Chalice | 2006 ▶
10 x 3 inches
(25.4 x 7.6 cm)
Beech, rose thorns
Photo by artist

◀ **Tea Time?** | 1995
4 x 5 inches
(10.2 x 12.7 cm)
Cherry, rose thorns
Photo by Michael Siede

DAVID SENGEL

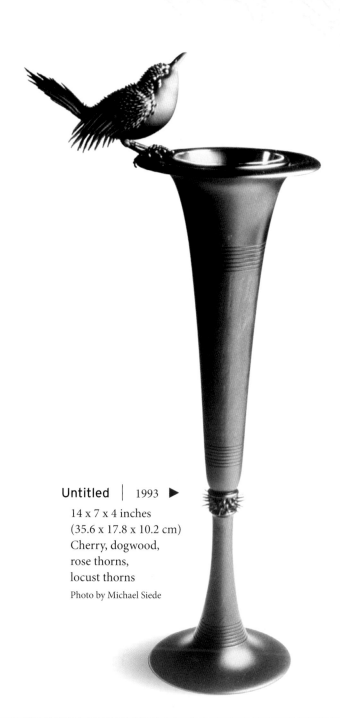

Untitled | 1993 ▶

14 x 7 x 4 inches
(35.6 x 17.8 x 10.2 cm)
Cherry, dogwood,
rose thorns,
locust thorns

Photo by Michael Siede

▲ **On the Fence** | 2003

17 x 15 x 4 inches
(43.2 x 38.1 x 10.2 cm)
Various woods

Photo by Troy Tuttle

DAVID **SENGEL**

◀ **Fish Sandwich** | 2004

4 x 16 x 9 inches
(10.2 x 40.6 x 22.9 cm)
Quilted maple, curly maple

Photo by Troy Tuttle

◀ **Peace Meal** | 2004

5 x 15 x 10 inches
(12.7 x 38.1 x 25.4 cm)
Buckeye burl, rose thorns,
locust thorns

Photo by Troy Tuttle

" For me, woodturning has evolved from an exploration of the vessel form through the addition of textural techniques and the use of found objects. These days, the lathe isn't always the primary tool in my studio. "

▲ Sylvan Plane | 1991

9 x 18 x 12 inches
(22.9 x 45.7 x 30.5 cm)
Maple burl, locust thorns

Photo by Michael Siede

Alan Stirt

EXEMPLIFYING THE CONCEPT THAT LESS IS MORE, Alan Stirt's bowls are subtle and understated, yet they command attention. Using shape, color, and texture to reinforce each other, Stirt achieves a balance between these elements so that each has equal weight in his work. He views the turning process as an exploration of the expressive possibilities of traditional forms. Carving and painting are central parts of his creative process, and pattern is a prime concern. Stirt uses patterns, whether created by grain structure, organic fluting and carving, or repeated geometric shapes, to develop harmony in each of his pieces. His square bowls are created from roughly rectangular blocks of wood. His large-rimmed, carved platters use the rim as a canvas—part of the total composition of the piece. Characterized by a simple elegance and integrity of design, Stirt's work has a unique classical purity.

▲ **Bowl with Coves** | 2002
5 x 13 inches
(12.7 x 33 cm)
Curly maple
Photo by artist

▲ Faceted Bowl | 2005

8 x 6½ inches
(20.3 x 16.5 cm)
Mesquite

Photo by artist

◀ **Square Ceremonial Bowl** | 2004

24 x 26 x 2 inches
(61 x 66 x 5.1 cm)
Mahogany
Photo by artist

" When my students ask for a recipe for creativity and good design,
I tell them I don't have one. The best I can do is cultivate an open
awareness of what works and what doesn't work in a piece. "

◀ **Ripple Pattern Platter** | 2006

14 x 16 x 2½ inches
(35.6 x 40.6 x 6.4 cm)
Black cherry
Photo by artist

Textured Square Bowl | 2005 ▶

1½ x 6 x 5 inches
(3.8 x 15.2 x 12.7 cm)
Tulipwood
Photo by artist

ALAN STIRT

" The longer I work, the more I realize the value of 'rough edges'—the unplanned elements that can make a piece come alive, or kill it completely. "

Crowded Square Bowl | 1998 ▶
14 x 2¼ inches
(35.6 x 5.7 cm)
Sugar maple
Photo by artist

Tidal Rip Platter | 1995 ▶
19 x 2 inches
(48.3 x 5.1 cm)
Black cherry
Photo by artist

▲ **Circles** │ 1998

16 x 2½ inches
(40.6 x 6.4 cm)
Sugar maple
Photo by artist

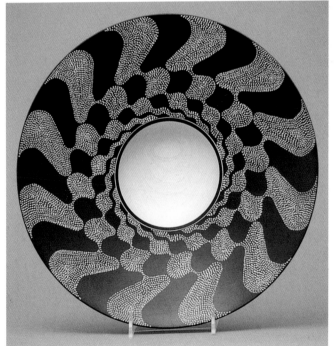

▲ **Transforming Wave Bowl** │ 1999

16 x 2½ inches
(40.6 x 6.4 cm)
Sugar maple
Photo by artist

▲ **Box Elder African Series Bowl** | 1990

7⅝ x 6 inches
(19.4 x 15.2 cm)
Box elder burl

Photo by artist

◀ **Bowl with Woven Texture** | 2002

    4 x 7 inches
    (10.2 x 17.8 cm)
    Boxwood
    Photo by artist

▲ **Nairobi Squares Platter** | 2007

    2 x 17 inches
    (5.1 x 43.2 cm)
    Mahogany
    Photo by artist

ALAN STIRT

Michael Brolly

CHARACTERIZED BY A UNIQUE COMBINATION of whimsicality and craftsmanship, the work of Michael Brolly is in a class by itself. His complex assemblages of pieces serve as ironic, humorous sculptures while showcasing his skills as an artist. Brolly has developed his own methods for working with wood. He often begins a new piece by carving a bas relief into the form, then sandblasting away the summer wood. His special sandblasting technique creates an optical illusion in the material, resulting in a form that resembles a hologram. Like a good poet, Brolly uses symbolism sparingly, giving viewers just enough detail so that they can reflect on their own experiences and extract meaning from his work. His innovative pieces have expanded our conception of the ways in which woodturned objects can express feelings and ideas. Beautiful in form and workmanship, his work is never less than compelling thanks to its complexity and use of humor.

◀ www.jewel@space.re | 1998

Each, 59 x 16 x 20 inches
(149.9 x 40.6 x 50.8 cm)
Mahogany, maple, purpleheart
Photos by David Haas

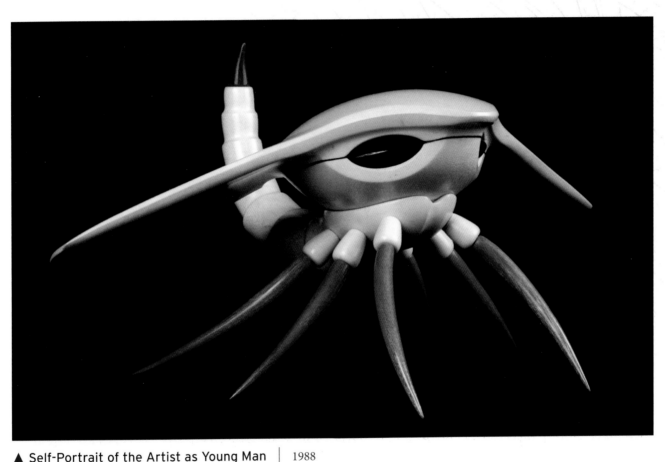

▲ **Self-Portrait of the Artist as Young Man** | 1988

27 x 16 x 10 inches (68.6 x 40.6 x 25.4 cm)
Lacewood, maple, mahogany, ebony

Photo by David Haas

▲ **Mother/Daughter, Hunter/Prey #2** │ 1992

Tallest, 6 x 13 x 13 inches
(15.2 x 33 x 33 cm)
Mahogany, purpleheart,
maple, ebony, budinga

Photo by David Haas

Bad Seed │ 2002 ▶

22 x 14 x 8 inches
(55.9 x 35.6 x 20.3 cm)
Maple, holly, ebony

Photo by David Haas

◀ Baron Von Baseball | 1997

4 x 8 x 7 inches
(10.2 x 20.3 x 17.8 cm)
Ash, walnut, cherry

Photo by David Haas

A Couple of Frog Bowls | 1988 and 1992 ▼

Tallest, 5 x 4 x 8 inches
(12.7 x 10.2 x 20.3 cm)
Maple, mahogany, ebony

Photo by David Haas

Soup Pot | 2007 ▶

12 x 6 inches
(30.5 x 15.2 cm)
Maple, Douglas fir
Photo by Eden Reiner

" I've used all kinds of lathes, from pedal lathes to

pattern-maker's lathes, and there is something

so immediate, so thrilling in the work. I've never

really been able to put it into words. "

◄ **Apron Tea Cup** | 2007

5 x 2½ inches
(12.7 x 6.4 cm)
Maple, Douglas fir
Photo by Eden Reiner

Cross Bowl | 2007 ►

8¼ x 1½ inches
(21 x 3.8 cm)
Maple, Douglas fir
Photo by Eden Reiner

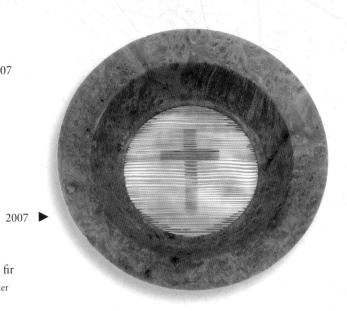

◄ **Plates** | 2007

11¼ x 1 inches
(28.6 x 2.5 cm)
Maple, Douglas fir
Photo by Eden Reiner

MICHAEL **BROLLY**

" Sometimes my work is just about the joke, but at other times there's a deeper meaning that I am trying to get at. "

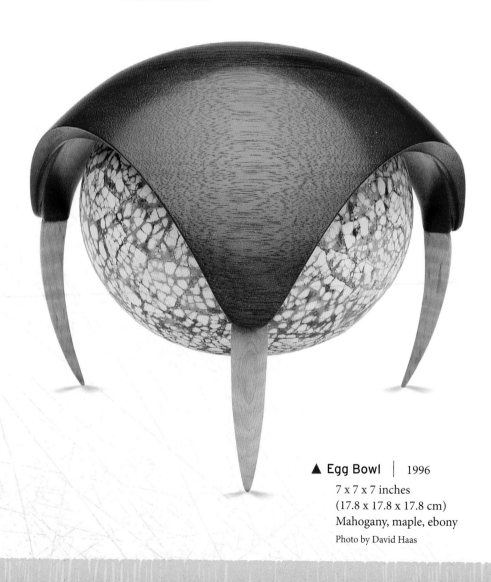

▲ Egg Bowl | 1996
7 x 7 x 7 inches
(17.8 x 17.8 x 17.8 cm)
Mahogany, maple, ebony
Photo by David Haas

◀ **Thinking of My Mother-in-Law Marianne and Those Magnificent Mahogany Breasts** | 1996

59 x 28 x 20 inches (149.9 x 71.1 x 50.8 cm)

Mahogany, maple, ebony, cherry

Photos by David Haas

MICHAEL **BROLLY**

Bill Luce

CONSTANTLY PUSHING THE ENVELOPE with his cutting and shaping techniques, Bill Luce is a perfectionist whose work emphasizes the timeless beauty of the bowl form. He takes advantage of the natural distortion of fresh green wood as it dries to alter and enhance the shape of each piece. Luce's objective is minimalism. His pieces are clean, pure, and streamlined. Because he strives to simplify his designs through refinement, he often creates work in a series in order to study nuances of shape and tactile balance. His work is a continuous exploration of form, within which lies yet another exploration—that of the interaction of the vessel shape with the visible elements of the wood. Although he sometimes enhances those elements through techniques such as sandblasting, Luce usually lets the wood speak for itself, without embellishment. The end result is never less than breathtaking.

▲ **Essence Series #3** | 2006

4½ x 8¼ x 13 inches
(11.4 x 21 x 33 cm)
Douglas fir
Photo by artist

▲ **Strata Series #3** | 2007

9¼ x 11½ x 11¾ inches
(23.5 x 29.2 x 29.8 cm)
Douglas fir

Photo by artist

▲ **Untitled** | 2005
6 x 10 inches
(15.2 x 25.4 cm)
Bigleaf maple
Photo by Jonathan McQuire

> " It's the overall statement of a piece that excites me. For some work, I prefer wood that's not so dramatic, as that starkness can enhance the power of certain forms. "

▲ **Entropy** | 2005

9½ x 13 x 14 inches
(24.1 x 33 x 35.6 cm)
Madrone burl

Photo by Jonathan McQuire

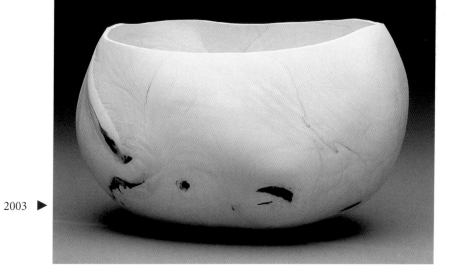

Lunar Landscapes in Holly, #3 | 2003 ▶

6½ x 11 inches (16.5 x 27.9 cm)
Holly

Photo by Mustafa Balil

▲ **Strata Series #1** | 2007

8 x 7½ inches
(20.3 x 19.1 cm)
Douglas fir
Photo by artist

" My primary focus is on exploring the subtleties of simple shape and form. My goal is to create vessels with a quiet yet powerful emotional impact. "

▲ **Untitled** │ 2005

4 x 6 inches
(10.2 x 15.2 cm)
Madrone
Photo by Jonathan McQuire

▲ **Untitled** │ 2006

4½ x 6 inches
(11.4 x 15.2 cm)
Oak
Photo by artist

◀ **Revelations** │ 2006

4½ x 6 inches
(11.4 x 15.2 cm)
Douglas fir
Photo by artist

" Many of my pieces have no separate foot. They rest, balanced, on a rounded lower portion. With no visual or tactile interruption from rim to rim, this type of form seems especially pure to me. "

▲ **Tsukiyomi no Kami** | 2005
4 x 5½ inches
(10.2 x 14 cm)
Elm
Photo by Mustafa Balil

◀ **Untitled** | 2006
3½ x 5¼ inches
(8.9 x 13.3 cm)
Bigleaf maple burl
Photo by artist

▲ **Selene** | 2002

4¾ x 6½ inches
(12.1 x 16.5 cm)
Holly

Photo by artist

Cindy Drozda

THE LIDDED VESSELS CREATED BY CINDY DROZDA were made to pique our curiosity. Look at these magical forms up close, and you experience the irresistible urge to lift the lid and peek inside. Drozda, who has been enchanted by the vessel form since childhood, creates perfectly proportioned pieces in which pattern and line work together synergistically. To imbue her work with a quality of motion, she turns her pieces thin, giving them a wonderful lightness. She pairs these fragile vessels with precisely formed finials and bases that she makes by hand. When viewed from a distance, Drozda's work appears to float on air. Working with the burl is a process she compares to working with a geode: There is no way to know beforehand what the material will look like inside. Each cut is final, but each cut reveals a hidden treasure.

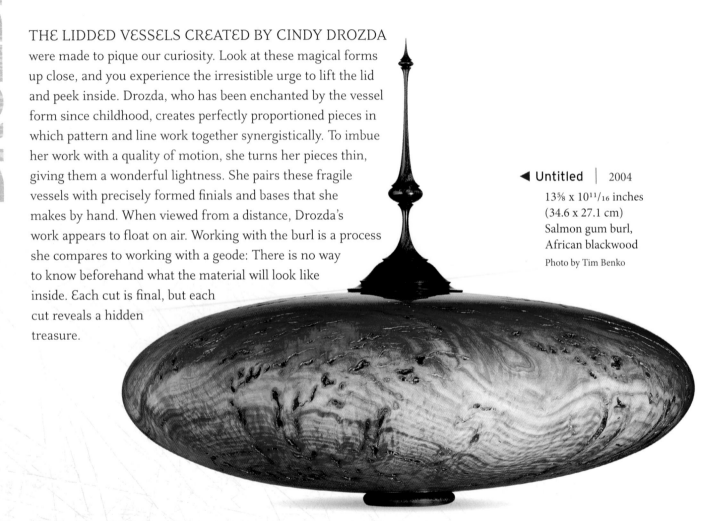

◀ **Untitled** │ 2004

13⅝ x 10¹¹/₁₆ inches
(34.6 x 27.1 cm)
Salmon gum burl,
African blackwood

Photo by Tim Benko

▲ **Green Oyster** | 2005

8½ x 5⁹/₁₆ inches
(21.6 x 14.1 cm)
Chechen burl,
African blackwood

Photo by Tim Benko

8³/₁₆ x 8 inches
(20.8 x 20.3 cm)
Eucalyptus gum vein burl,
African blackwood

Photo by Tim Benko

" I choreograph the burl figure
with the vessel form to show it
to its best advantage. "

Demeter | 2005 ▶

16¹³/₁₆ x 6¹³/₁₆ inches
(42.8 x 17.3 cm)
Eucalyptus gum vein burl,
African blackwood

Photo by Tim Benko

CINDY DROZDA

◀ **Untitled** | 2004

15 x 5⅝ inches
(38.1 x 14.3 cm)
Amboyna burl,
African blackwood

Photo by Tim Benko

▲ **Space Station** | 2004

7 x 3½ inches
(17.8 x 8.9 cm)
Banksia seed pod

Photo by Tim Benko

◀ **Untitled** | 2004

14⅜ x 6 inches
(36.6 x 15.2 cm)
Chechen burl,
African blackwood

Photo by Tim Benko

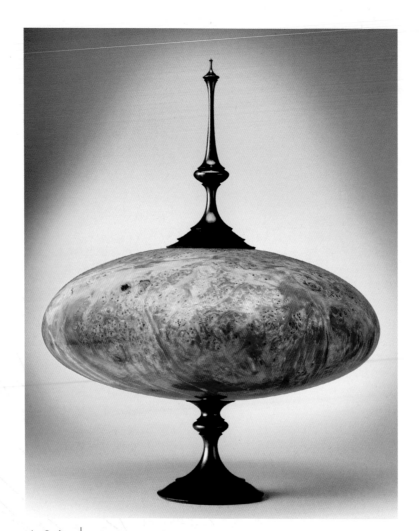

▲ Gaia | 2006
14¹³/₁₆ x 11¹¹/₁₆ inches
(37.7 x 29 cm)
Tasmanian myrtle burl,
African blackwood
Photo by Tim Benko

" The lidded vessel is a composition of elements,

very much like a musical composition. "

▲ Sunset | 2006

8¹³/₁₆ x 11¹¹/₁₆ inches
(22.4 x 29 cm)
Box elder burl,
African blackwood

Photo by Tim Benko

▲ **The Unununium Conundrum** | 2007

11 x 11½ inches
(27.9 x 29.2 cm)
Box elder burl,
African blackwood
Photo by Tim Benko

Yemaya | 2005 ▶

15¹¹/₁₆ x 6½ inches
(39.8 x 16.5 cm)
Amboyna burl,
African blackwood
Photo by Tim Benko

" When I create a lidded vessel, I like to hide a secret treasure inside, a secret that's available only to the person who's bold enough to lift the lid. This hidden detail symbolizes for me the treasure that life reveals when we make the effort to look deeper within. "

◀ **Untitled** | 2003
9 x 11 inches
(22.9 x 27.9 cm)
Jarrah burl,
African blackwood
Photos by Tim Benko

Michael Lee

WHEN YOU LOOK AT THE WORK OF MICHAEL LEE, you feel you're observing a new species of marine life. A native of Hawaii, Lee has been heavily influenced by island culture, and it shows in his work. Fish, shell, and water imagery permeate his pieces, which are infused with a sense of motion and fluidity. His sculptural vessels include shell-like objects that have a unique kind of energy. With their expertly designed whorls and angles, these pieces resemble living, breathing sea creatures. Other pieces have the look of ocean vegetation. Featuring complex patterns and textures, Lee's work is incredibly detailed. Tiny starfish, finely etched scales, rippling waves—all are rendered with precision and integrity. Despite its inherent artfulness, Lee's work feels undeniably organic, characterized by a harmonious marriage between texture, color, and form.

Gray-Haired Tako | 1999 ▶

4½ x 8 x 8 inches
(11.4 x 20.3 x 20.3 cm)
Pheasant wood

Photo by Hugo de Vries

▲ **Hoku** | 2005

3 x 5 x 6 inches
(7.6 x 12.7 x 15.2 cm)
Gabon ebony

Photo by Hugo de Vries

◀ **Armored Crab** | 1998

2¾ x 5¼ x 5¼ inches
(7 x 13.3 x 13.3 cm)
Kingwood

Photo by Hugo de Vries

◀ **Crab's Nest** | 2005

3 x 5 x 6 inches
(7.6 x 12.7 x 15.2 cm)
Gabon ebony,
yellowheart

Photos by Hugo de Vries

▲ Lagoons | 1999

6 x 9 x 9 inches
(15.2 x 22.9 x 22.9 cm)
Milo

Photo by Hugo de Vries

Ebb and Flow | 2002 ▶

3 x 9½ x 9 inches
(7.6 x 24.1 x 22.9 cm)
Milo

Photo by Hugo de Vries

MICHAEL LEE

◀ **Ipu Pod** | 2000

7 x 6 x 6 inches
(17.8 x 15.2 x 15.2 cm)
Koa

Photos by Hugo de Vries

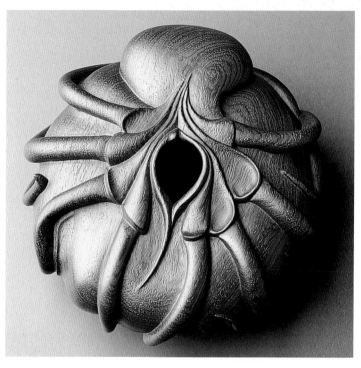

> **"** When I start a new piece, things often don't go the way I planned initially. I call these moments 'design detours,' because I need to find another path to follow. Eventually, I find an alternate route on my way to completion. **"**

◀ **Takobolo** | 1996
4½ x 8 x 8 inches
(11.4 x 20.3 x 20.3 cm)
Cocobolo, rosewood
Photo by Hugo de Vries

Ammonite Pod | 2000 ▶
5½ x 6½ x 8½ inches
(14 x 16.5 x 21.6 cm)
Kamani

Photos by Hugo de Vries

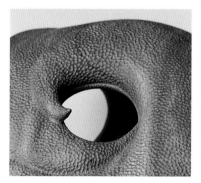

" Growing up in a Chinese household, I was
surrounded by beautiful vases and carvings
made of wood and ivory. I always marveled
at their craftsmanship. These pieces led me
to the path I'm now on. "

Nalu Pod │ 2002 ▶

3 x 9¼ x 7½ inches
(7.6 x 23.5 x 19.1 cm)
Koa

Photo by Hugo de Vries

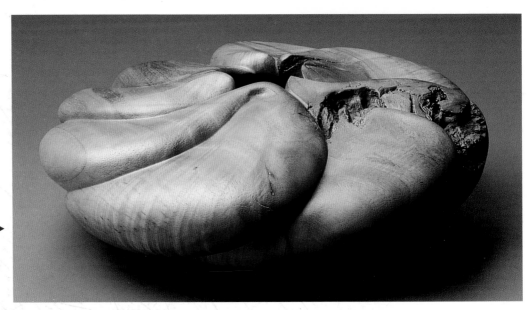

Pod Form │ 1996 ▶

4 x 11 x 11 inches
(10.2 x 27.9 x 27.9 cm)
Koa

Photo by Hugo de Vries

MICHAEL LEE

▲ **Ammonite Pod** | 2003

    7 x 8¼ x 4¼ inches
    (17.8 x 21 x 10.8 cm)
    Cocobolo, rosewood
    Photo by Hugo de Vries

About the Curator

A fascination with the process of design has led Jim Christiansen to explore woodturning and creativity. Many of his current activities focus on broadening the awareness of design principles within the woodturning community. Following this path, he has produced a unique variety of work that has received widespread attention. Christiansen's creations have been featured in magazines and books such as *American Woodturner* and *Wood Art Today*. He has exhibited nationally and internationally and traveled extensively, teaching others about critique and design. He has curated a number of regional shows and several major exhibitions, including Woodturning on the Edge in 2006, which featured groundbreaking work by leading turners. Christiansen believes his most important role is that of mentor. He spends a lot of time in his Moscow, Idaho, studio working with individuals who want to learn more about art and design.

▲ **Feeling is Believing** | 2007

15 x 14 x 5 inches (38 x 35.5 x 12.7 cm)
Maple

Photo by Archer Photography

Portrait Photographers

Thank you to the photographers whose portraits of the woodturning artists appear in this book:

Brenda Behrens, photo by DV Sundberg Photography
Betty Scarpino, photo by Shawn Spence
Christian Burchard, photo by Liz Ellingson
Don Derry, photo by Zane Kinney
Cindy Drozda, photo by Tim Benko
Jean-François Escoulen, photo by Yves Duble
Stephen Hogbin, photo by Michael McLuhan
Michelle Holzapfel, photo by David Holzapfel
Michael Lee, photo by Doug Young
Bert Marsh, photo by Mary Marsh

The photos of Michael Bauermeister, Michael Brolly, Marilyn Campbell, Ben Carpenter, David Ellsworth, J. Paul Fennell, Ron Fleming, Clay Foster, Ron Gerton, Giles Gilson, Stephen Hatcher, Michael Hosaluk, William Hunter, John Jordan, Bud Latven, Ron Layport, Bill Luce, Alain Mailland, Hugh McKay, William Moore, Binh Pho, Graeme Priddle, David Sengel, Mark Sfirri, Steve Sinner, Alan Stirt, Malcolm Tibbetts, Gerrit Van Ness, Jacques Vesery, and Hans Weissflog are self-portraits.

Acknowledgments

Grateful appreciation goes out to the artists whose amazing work and words grace these pages. I am in awe of what wood speaks in the hands of such skilled craftspersons. Our sincere thanks also to the insightful, discerning Jim Christiansen, who selected the most remarkable group possible to represent the best in contemporary woodturning. His vision, more than any other thing, shaped this book's content. Lark staff members took the raw material of images and writing and gave them a final polish. Cassie Moore and Dawn Dillingham tracked every piece of information and imagery—a huge job—and Julie Hale did the lion's share editorially. Chris Rich did a wonderful job of proofreading the text. Our art production staff, headed up by Shannon Yokeley, herded cats when the book's visual parts arrived. Jeff Hamilton and Megan Kirby skillfully brought all these elements together into the beautiful package you hold in your hands.

—*Suzanne J. E. Tourtillott, Senior Editor*

Artist Index